Baby Names

The Ultimate Baby Names Guide with Thousands of Names with Meaning and Origin

Contents

Acknowledgements

The creation of this book has been a long process. We had to go through hundreds of databases in order to compile our own database with only the best names. We would like to thank Louis Kalahan, Roger Stone, and Owen Hudson for being so grateful with your time. Without you guys, this book wouldn't exist.

Also, to our kids Steve, John, and Melissa, we would like to say thank you! You are our deepest motivation. Our fantastic parents are also very much appreciated and loved. And of course, thanks to all the business associates who have been supporting from the start! It took us two years to create this book, but without all of the aboves help; we don't think that the book would be alive.

Introduction

Finding a name for your baby can be a long and frustrating process. There are so many things to think about and so little time. Why can't the name just fall out of the sky or be given by God as it is in some movies? *If only there was a simple way of finding the perfect name for my baby.*

If this thought has crossed your mind, worry no more! With the help of this book, we doubt that you will have any difficulty in regards to finding the perfect name. In this book, you will find thousands of names with meaning and origin. Some you will adore, and some you will not, but see this process of searching as a gold miner does. You have to cut through some stone in order to get to the gold.

At the end of the book, you will get a checklist so you can test to see if you have found the right one.

So, without further ado, shall we get started?

Chapter 1 – The Most Popular Boy Names in 2017

- **Logan**, Origin: Celtic, Meaning: Little hollow
- **Oliver**, Origin: German, Meaning: Olive tree
- **Nicholas**, Origin: Greek, Meaning: People of Victory
- **Wyatt**, Origin: English, Meaning: Brave in war
- **Bryson**, Origin: Welsh, Meaning: Son of Brice
- **Christian**, Origin: Latin, Meaning: Follower of Christ
- **Jaxon**, Origin: Greek, Meaning: Jack's son
- **Joshua**, Origin: Hebrew, Meaning: The Lord is my salvation
- **Mason**, Origin: French, Meaning: Stoneworker
- **Alexander**, Origin: Greek, Meaning: Defending men
- **Kayden**, Origin: Celtic, Meaning: Battle, Son of Cadan
- **Ryan**, Origin: Celtic, Meaning: Little king
- **Cameron**, Origin: Celtic, Meaning: Bent nose
- **Ayden**, Origin: Celtic, Meaning: Little fire

- **Ian**, Origin: Hebrew, Meaning: The Lord is gracious
- **Aiden**, Origin: Celtic, Meaning: Fiery and little
- **Christopher,** Origin: Greek, Meaning: Bearer of Christ
- **John**, Origin: Hebrew, Meaning: God is gracious
- **Dominic**, Origin: Latin, Meaning: Belonging to the lord
- **Elias**, Origin: Hebrew, Meaning: My God is the lord
- **Carson**, Origin: Celtic, Meaning: Son of the marsh dwellers
- **Zachary**, Origin: Hebrew, Meaning: The Lord has remembered
- **Bentley**, Origin: English, Meadow with coarse grass
- **Jack**, Origin: English, Meaning: God is gracious
- **Easton**, Origin: English, Meaning: East facing place
- **Carter,** Origin: English, Meaning: Driver or cart maker
- **Jackson**, Origin: English, Meaning: Son of Jack

- **Jason**, Origin: Greek, Meaning: To heal
- **Hudson**, Origin: English, Meaning: Son of Hugh
- **Jacob**, Origin: Hebrew, Meaning: Supplanter
- **Sebastian**, Origin: German, Meaning: From the ancient city of Sebasta
- **Eli,** Origin: Hebrew, Meaning: Ascended, high, uplifted
- **Leonardo**, Origin: German, Meaning: Brave lion
- **Cooper**, Origin: English, Meaning: Barrel maker
- **Jayden**, Origin: Hebrew, Meaning: God has heard
- **Liam**, Origin: German, Meaning: Resolute protection
- **Jose**, Origin: Spanish, Meaning: Jehovah increases
- **Roman**, Origin: Latin, Meaning: Citizen of Rome
- **David**, Origin: Hebrew, Meaning: Beloved
- **Noah**, Origin: Hebrew, Meaning: Comfort, Rest

- **Anthony**, Origin: English, Meaning: Priceless one
- **Isaac**, Origin: Hebrew, Meaning: Laughter
- **Landon**, Origin: English, Meaning: Long hill
- **Jace**, Origin: Greek, Meaning: Moon-Var. of Jason
- **Andrew**, Origin: Greek, Meaning: Manly and strong
- **Daniel,** Origin: Hebrew, Meaning: God is my judge
- **Benjamin,** Origin: Hebrew, Meaning: Son of the right hand
- **Michael**, Origin: Hebrew, Meaning: Who is like God?
- **Ethan,** Origin: Hebrew, Meaning: Firm, strong
- **Elijah**, Origin: Hebrew, Meaning: Yahweh is God
- **Aaron**, Origin: Hebrew, Meaning: High mountain; enlightened, exalted
- **Henry**, Origin: German, Meaning: Estate ruler
- **Owen**, Origin: Welsh, Meaning: Well-born; young warrior
- **Angel**, Origin: Greek, Meaning: Word name
- **Hunter**, Origin: English, Meaning: One who hunts

- **Santiago**, Origin: Latin, Meaning: Saint James
- **William**, Origin: German, Meaning: Resolute protection
- **Isaiah**, Origin: Hebrew, Meaning: Salvation of the Lord
- **Thomas**, Origin: Aramaic, Meaning: Twin
- **Jeremiah**, Origin: Hebrew, Meaning: Appointed by God
- **Jaxson**, Origin: English, Meaning: Jack's son
- **Robert**, Origin: German, Meaning: Bright fame
- **Parker**, Origin: French, Meaning: Park keeper
- **Caleb**, Origin: Hebrew, Meaning: Devotion to God
- **Grayson**, Origin: English, Meaning: The son of the baliff
- **Mateo**, Origin: Hebrew, Meaning: Gift of God
- **Nathan**, Origin: Hebrew, Meaning: Given
- **Gavin**, Origin: Welsh, Meaning: White hawk
- **Leo**, Origin: Latin, Meaning: Lion
- **Lincoln**, Origin: English, Meaning: Town by the pool

- **Colton**, Origin: English, Meaning: From the coal or dark town
- **Tyler**, Origin: English, Meaning: Maker of tiles
- **Dylan**, Origin: Welsh, Meaning: Son of the sea
- **Jordan**, Origin: Hebrew, Meaning: Flowing down
- **Connor**, Origin: Celtic, Meaning: Lover of hounds
- **Gabriel**, Origin: Hebrew, Meaning: God is my strenght
- **Matthew**, Origin: Hebrew, Meaning: Gift of God
- **Brayden**, Origin: Celtic, Meaning: Broad hill
- **Luke**, Origin: Greek, Meaning: Man from Luciana
- **Lucas**, Origin: Latin, Meaning: Man from Luciana
- **Charles**, Origin: German, Meaning: Free man
- **James,** Origin: Hebrew, Meaning: Supplanter
- **Greyson**, Origin: English, Meaning: Son of the steward
- **Chase**, Origin: English, Meaning: To hunt
- **Brandon,** Origin: English, Meaning: Broom-covered hill

- **Kevin**, Origin: Celtic, Meaning: Handsome
- **Levi**, Origin: Hebrew, Meaning: Attached, joined
- **Josiah**, Origin: Hebrew, Meaning: Heals, God supports
- **Jonathan**, Origin: Hebrew, Meaning: Gift of Jehovah
- **Nolan**, Origin: Celtic, Meaning: Champion
- **Joseph,** Origin: Hebrew, Meaning: Jehovah increases
- **Austin**, Origin: Latin, Meaning: Magnificent, Great
- **Ezra,** Origin: Hebrew, Meaning: Helper
- **Adam,** Origin: Hebrew, Meaning: Son of the red earth
- **Adrian**, Origin: Latin, Meaning: Man of Adria
- **Asher,** Origin: Hebrew, Meaning: Happy one, Fortunate, Blessed
- **Samuel,** Origin: Hebrew, Meaning: Told by God
- **Julian,** Origin: Latin, Meaning: Downy, Youthful
- **Xavier**, Origin: Basque, Meaning: Bright or new house

- **Evan,** Origin: Hebrew, Meaning: The lord is gracious

Chapter 2 – Boy Names Sorted By Different Meanings

These names below are sorted by different meanings. The meaning is located at the top of each subsequent list. Each list is also sorted from Z-A.

Gift of God

- ➤ **Theodore,** Origin: Greek
- ➤ **Teodoro,** Origin: Greek, Italian
- ➤ **Nathaniel,** Origin: Hebrew
- ➤ **Mattie**, Origin: English, Teutonic, German, Hebrew
- ➤ **Matthew,** Origin: Hebrew
- ➤ **Mathias,** Origin: Hebrew, Swedish
- ➤ **Jonathan,** Origin: Hebrew

Man:

- **Marques,** Origin: Spanish, Portuguese
- **Manzie,** Origin: American
- **Manny,** Origin: Spanish, English
- **Manning,** Origin: English
- **Manley,** Origin: English
- **Manfred,** Origin: Teutonic, English
- **Macleod**, Origin: English, Gaelic
- **Mackean,** Origin: Scottish
- **Lenno,** Origin: Native American
- **Karl**, Origin: Teutonic, German
- **Kale**, Origin: Hawaiian
- **Jove,** Origin: Latin, Greek
- **Jerry**, Origin: Greek, English, German
- **Jermaine**, Origin: Latin
- **Jarvis**, Origin: English, Old English, German
- **Janus**, Origin: Latin
- **Ibrahim**, Origin: Arabic, Hebrew
- **Howard**, Origin: English, Old English
- **Gregory**, Origin: Greek, Latin

- **Gregor,** Origin: Greek, Dutch
- **German**, Origin: Spanish, French, English
- **Germaine**, Origin: French
- **Gerardo**, Origin: Spanish, German
- **Gerard,** Origin: Teutonic, English
- **Gavrie,** Origin: Russian
- **Gatlin**, Origin: English
- **Garrett**, Origin: English, Old German, Irish
- **Freeman,** Origin: English
- **Francesco**, Origin: Latin, Italian
- **Foster**, Origin: English
- **Forsythe**, Origin: Gaelic
- **Flynn**, Origin: Celtic, Irish
- **Fisher**, Origin: English, Old English
- **Fabrizio**, Origin: Italian
- **Fabrice,** Origin: Italian
- **Eugenie**, Origin: Greek
- **Eugene**, Origin: Greek
- **Ellsworth**, Origin: Hebrew, English
- **Edgar,** Origin: English, Old English
- **Earl,** Origin: Celtic, English, Old English
- **Duke**, Origin: English, French
- **Destry**, Origin: French, English
- **Desmond**, Origin: Celtic, Irish, Gaelic

- **Dermot,** Origin: Celtic, Irish
- **Declan**, Origin: Celtic, Gaelic, Irish
- **Charles**, Origin: Teutonic, Old German, German
- **Cartman**, Origin: English
- **Carl**, Origin: English, Teutonic, Old German, German
- **Bwana**, Origin: Swahili
- **Butch,** Origin: American
- **Bono,** Origin: Latin
- **Bolton**, Origin: English
- **Armando,** Origin: Teutonic, German, Spanish
- **Armand**, Origin: Teutonic, German
- **Archer,** Origin: English
- **Apollo,** Origin: Greek
- **Ansel**, Origin: French, German
- **Andrew**, Origin: Greek
- **Andreas**, Origin: Teutonic, Greek
- **Anders,** Origin: Greek, Scandinavian
- **Almanzo**, Origin: Old German
- **Alexander,** Origin: Greek
- **Adam**, Origin: Hebrew
- **Abraham,** Origin: Hebrew
- **Marquis,** Origin: French
- **Medgar**, Origin: German
- **Oscar,** Origin: English, Old English, Scandinavian

- **Paine**, Origin: Latin
- **Patrick,** Origin: Latin
- **Pompey**, Origin: Latin
- **Quenby,** Origin: Scandinavian
- **Quimby,** Origin: Scandinavian
- **Richard**, Origin: English, Old German
- **Rodman,** Origin: English, German
- **Roger**, Origin: English, Old German, German
- **Romany**, Origin: Romany
- **Rutger**, Origin: Dutch, Scandinavian
- **Ryder**, Origin: English, Old English
- **Saxon,** Origin: English
- **Steadman**, Origin: English
- **Thurgood,** Origin: English
- **Truman,** Origin: English
- **Wayman**, Origin: English
- **Wentworth**, Origin: English
- **Whit**, Origin: English
- **Whitman,** Origin: English
- **Yancey**, Origin: Native American

Sun

- **Sundance,** Origin: American
- **Ravi,** Origin: Hindi
- **Sulwen**, Origin: Welsh
- **Dayton**, Origin: English, Old English
- **Shadow,** Origin: English
- **Sargon,** Origin: Persian
- **Aditya**, Origin: Native American, Indian, Sanskrit
- **Cyrus**, Origin: Persian
- **Sula**, Origin: Norse, Scandinavian

Strong

- **Willard,** Origin: Teutonic, German
- **Valery,** Origin: Russian, Latin
- **Valerie,** Origin: French, Latin
- **Valeria,** Origin: Italian, Latin
- **Valentino**, Origin: Italian
- **Valentin**, Origin: Spanish, Latin
- **Richmond,** Origin: Teutonic, German
- **Remo**, Origin: English, Greek
- **Raynor**, Origin: English, Scandinavian
- **Ragnar,** Origin: English, Scandinavian
- **Quinlan,** Origin: Celtic, Irish
- **Quigley,** Origin: Celtic, Irish
- **Plato**, Origin: Greek
- **Neon,** Origin: Greek
- **Kwan,** Origin: Chinese, Korean
- **Kemen**, Origin: Spanish, Basque
- **Humberto**, Origin: Teutonic, Portuguese
- **Gerrit**, Origin: Teutonic, Dutch
- **Fergus**, Origin: Celtic, Irish
- **Ezra**, Origin: Hebrew
- **Ethan**, Origin: Hebrew
- **Etai**, Origin: Hebrew

- **Emmett**, Origin: English, German
- **Ellard**, Origin: Teutonic, German
- **Ekon,** Origin: Nigerian
- **Eberhard,** Origin: Teutonic, German
- **Durell**, Origin: English, French
- **Djimon**, Origin: West African
- **Charlie,** Origin: Teutonic, Old German, German
- **Charles,** Origin: Teutonic, Old German, German
- **Brian,** Origin: Celtic, Irish, Scottish
- **Bogart,** Origin: Teutonic, French
- **Boaz,** Origin: Hebrew
- **Barrett**, Origin: English, German
- **Armstrong**, Origin: English
- **Andrew,** Origin: Greek
- **Andreas,** Origin: Teutonic, Greek
- **Andrea**, Origin: Greek
- **Anders**, Origin: Greek, Scandinavian

Warrior

- **Wyman,** Origin: English
- **Wyatt**, Origin: English, Old English, French
- **Tupac**, Origin: Aztec
- **Tennessee,** Origin: American, Cherokee
- **Steinar**, Origin: Norwegian
- **Sloan**, Origin: Celtic, Irish
- **Rogelio**, Origin: Spanish
- **Raynor**, Origin: English, Scandinavian
- **Ragnar**, Origin: English, Scandinavian
- **Peyton,** Origin: English, Old English
- **Patton**, Origin: English
- **Owen**, Origin: Irish, Celtic, Welsh
- **Osborne**, Origin: Hebrew, English
- **Murphy**, Origin: Celtic
- **Morrow**, Origin: English
- **Mars,** Origin: Latin
- **Luther**, Origin: Teutonic, German
- **Lute**, Origin: Hebrew, English
- **Louis,** Origin: Teutonic, French, German
- **Knight**, Origin: English
- **Kimball**, Origin: English
- **Killian**, Origin: Celtic, Irish
- **Kelly,** Origin: Celtic, Irish

- **Kellen**, Origin: Celtic, Irish
- **Keely**, Origin: Celtic, Gaelic, Irish
- **Kael,** Origin: Celtic, Irish
- **Gerald**, Origin: Teutonic, Old German, German
- **Evan,** Origin: Hebrew, Irish, Celtic
- **Edwidge**, Origin: English
- **Duncan**, Origin: Celtic, Scottish
- **Donovan**, Origin: Celtic, Irish
- **Clovis**, Origin: Teutonic, French
- **Chad**, Origin: English, Old English
- **Calhoun**, Origin: Celtic, Irish
- **Cadman**, Origin: Celtic, Irish
- **Boris**, Origin: Russian, Slavic
- **Bellatrix**, Origin: Latin
- **Aryan**, Origin: Latin
- **Ajax**, Origin: Greek

King

- **Waverly**, Origin: English
- **Wassili,** Origin: Greek
- **Ryne,** Origin: American, Irish
- **Ryan**, Origin: Celtic, Irish
- **Roy**, Origin: Celtic, Irish, French
- **Reynolds**, Origin: Celtic, English
- **Reynaldo**, Origin: Teutonic, Spanish
- **Rey**, Origin: French, Spanish
- **Rex**, Origin: Latin
- **Ray**, Origin: French, Old German
- **Prince,** Origin: Latin
- **Pomeroy**, Origin: French
- **Pippin,** Origin: French, German
- **Obba**, Origin: Yoruban
- **Naresh,** Origin: Indian, Hindi
- **Melchior**, Origin: Arabic
- **Leroy**, Origin: French, Portuguese
- **LeBron**, Origin: African
- **Kinsley**, Origin: English, Celtic, American
- **Kingston,** Origin: English
- **Kingsley,** Origin: English
- **Kenwood**, Origin: English

- **Kendrick**, Origin: English, Welsh
- **Eze**, Origin: African
- **Elroy,** Origin: French
- **Delroy**, Origin: French
- **Common,** Origin: English
- **Basil,** Origin: Greek
- **Balthazar,** Origin: English, Greek
- **Ara**, Origin: Armenian, American, Arabic

Handsome

- **Yaphet**, Origin: Hebrew
- **Yamil,** Origin: Arabic
- **Yahir,** Origin: American, Arabic
- **Wasim,** Origin: Arabic
- **Shaquille**, Origin: African, Arabic
- **Kevin,** Origin: Celtic, Irish
- **Kenneth,** Origin: Celtic, Scottish, Irish
- **Kenna,** Origin: Celtic, Scottish, Irish
- **Keane**, Origin: English, Celtic
- **Kavanaugh**, Origin: Irish
- **Kavan**, Origin: Celtic, Irish
- **Japheth**, Origin: Hebrew
- **Jamir**, Origin: Arabic
- **Jamil**, Origin: Arabic
- **Jamel**, Origin: Arabic
- **Jamari**, Origin: French, Arabic
- **Jamar,** Origin: African, Arabic
- **Jamal,** Origin: Arabic
- **Hassan**, Origin: Arabic
- **Cullen**, Origin: Celtic, Irish

- **Cavan**, Origin: Celtic, Irish
- **Bello**, Origin: French
- **Beauregard**, Origin: French
- **Beau,** Origin: French
- **Alan,** Origin: Celtic, Old German, Irish

Chapter 3 – The Most Popular Girl Names in 2017

- **Eliana**, Origin: Hebrew, Meaning: My God has answered
- **Victoria**, Origin: Latin, Meaning: Victory
- **Faith**, Origin: English, Meaning: Belief, To trust
- **Harper**, Origin: English, Meaning: Harp player
- **Mila**, Origin: Slavic, Meaning: Diminutive of several European names
- **Penelope**, Origin: Greek, Meaning: Weaver
- **Olivia**, Origin: Latin, Meaning: Olive tree
- **Bella**, Origin: Latin, Meaning: Beautiful
- **Stella**, Origin: Latin, Meaning: Star
- **Autumn**, Origin: Latin, Meaning: Autumn
- **Allison**, Origin: German, Meaning: Noble
- **Eva**, Origin: Hebrew, Meaning: Life
- **Violet**, Origin: Latin, Meaning: Purple
- **Kaylee**, Origin: Celtic, Meaning: Laurel, Crown
- **Lily**, Origin: English, English, Meaning: flower name

- **Alyssa**, Origin: German, Meaning: Noble
- **Savannah**, Origin: English, Meaning: Flat tropical grassland
- **Madeline**, Origin: Hebrew, Meaning: Women from Magdala or high tower
- **Emilia**, Origin: Latin, Meaning: Rival; emulating (lating meaning). Industrious (Germanic meaning). Friendly; soft (Greek meaning).
- **Ashley**, Origin: English, Meaning: Dweller near the ash tree meadow
- **Grace**, Origin: Latin, Meaning: Grace of God, Beauty of form
- **Natalie**, Origin: Latin, Meaning: Birthday of the Lord
- **Maya**, Origin: Sanskrit, Meaning: Water
- **Hazel**, Origin: English, Meaning: The hazelnut tree
- **Lucy**, Origin: Latin, Meaning: Light
- **Emma**, Origin: Latin, Meaning: Universal
- **Trinity,** Origin: English, Meaning: Triad
- **Skylar**, Origin: Dutch, Meaning: Guarded, learned one (American meaning). Eternal life and strength (English meaning)
- **Emily,** Origin: Latin, Meaning: Rival

- **Lydia**, Origin: Greek, Meaning: Women from Lydia
- **Willow**, Origin: English, Meaning: Willow tree
- **Katherine**, Origin: Greek, Meaning: Pure
- **Alice**, Origin: German, Meaning: Noble
- **Liliana**, Origin: English, Meaning: To climb, like a vine
- **Julia**, Origin: Latin, Meaning: Youthful
- **Hailey**, Origin: English, Meaning: Hay's meadow
- **Ruby**, Origin: Latin, Meaning: Deep red precious stone
- **Layla**, Origin: Arabic, Meaning: Night
- **Audrey**, Origin: German, Meaning: Noble strenght
- **Aaliyah**, Origin: Hebrew, Meaning: Heavens, Exalted, Highborn
- **Sadie**, Origin: Hebrew, Meaning: Princess
- **Lillian**, Origin: Hebrew, Meaning: Lily, A Flower
- **Alexa**, Origin: Greek, Meaning: Defending men
- **Nora,** Origin: Latin, Meaning: Light

- **Camila,** Origin: French, Meaning: Young ceremonial attendant
- **Ella**, Origin: French, Meaning: Fairy maiden, All, Completly
- **Jasmine**, Origin: Persian, Meaning: Persian flowername
- **Hannah**, Origin: Hebrew, Meaning: Grace
- **Brianna**, Origin: Celtic, Meaning: Strong, honourable and virtuous
- **Kylie**, Origin: Celtic, Meaning: A boomerang
- **Amelia**, Origin: Hebrew, Meaning: Work
- **Aria**, Origin: Latin, Meaning: Air, Lioness
- **Brooklyn**, Origin: English, Meaning: Place-name
- **Jade**, Origin: Spanish, Meaning: Stone of the side
- **Serenity**, Origin: Latin, Meaning: Peaceful
- **Adeline**, Origin: English, Meaning: Noble, Nobility
- **Aubree**, Origin: French, Meaning: Elf ruler
- **Zoey**, Origin: Greek, Meaning: Life
- **Paisley**, Origin: Gaelic, Meaning: Church, cemetery
- **Isabella**, Origin: Hebrew, Meaning: Pledged to God

- **Anna,** Origin: Hebrew, Meaning: Grace
- **Natalia,** Origin: Latin, Meaning: Birthday of the Lord
- **Nevaeh**, Origin: English, Meaning: Modern invented name
- **Claire**, Origin: Latin, Meaning: Clear, bright
- **Leah,** Origin: Hebrew, Meaning: Weary
- **Valentina**, Origin: Latin, Meaning: Health, Strenght
- **Madclyn,** Origin: Hebrew, Meaning: High tower or women from Magdala
- **Madison**, Origin: English, Meaning: Son of Maud
- **Scarlett**, Origin: English, Meaning: Red
- **Sofia**, Origin: Greek, Meaning: Wisdom
- **Abigail,** Origin: Hebrew, Meaning: My father is joyful
- **Eleanor,** Origin: Hebrew, Meaning: Pity (Greek meaning). God is my light (Arabic meaning
- **Delilah,** Origin: Hebrew, Meaning: To flirt
- **Aurora,** Origin: Latin, Meaning: Dawn
- **Annabelle,** Origin: Italian, Meaning: Loving

- **Elena,** Origin: Greek, Meaning: Shining light, bright
- **Naomi**, Origin: Hebrew, Meaning: Pleasantness
- **Evelyn,** Origin: Celtic, Meaning: Wished for child
- **Ava**, Origin: Hebrew, Meaning: Life
- **Melanie**, Origin: Greek, Meaning: Dark, Black
- **Alexis,** Origin: Greek, Meaning: Defender
- **Piper**, Origin: English, Meaning: Flute player or piper
- **Isabelle**, Origin: Hebrew, Meaning: Pledged to God
- **Sarah**, Origin: Hebrew, Meaning: Princess
- **Ariana**, Origin: Welsh, Meaning: Most holy
- **Samantha**, Origin: English, Meaning: Told by God
- **Zoe**, Origin: Greek, Meaning: Life
- **Adalynn**, Origin: English, Meaning: Noble guardian
- **Arianna,** Origin: Greek, Meaning: Very holy one
- **Mia**, Origin: Latin, Meaning: Mine; bitter
- **Chloe,** Origin: Greek, Meaning: Young green shoot

- **Sophia**, Origin: Greek, Meaning: Wisdom
- **Gabriella,** Origin: Italian, Meaning: God is my strenght
- **Gianna**, Origin: Hebrew, Meaning: The Lord is gracious
- **Caroline**, Origin: German, Meaning: Free man
- **Luna**, Origin: Latin, Meaning: Moon
- **Charlotte**, Origin: Norse, Meaning: Free man
- **Ellie,** Origin: Hebrew, Meaning: Shining one, Bright
- **Athena**, Origin: Greek, Meaning: Greek Goddess of wisdom
- **Elizabeth**, Origin: Hebrew, Meaning: Pledged to God

Chapter 4 – Girl Names Sorted By Different Meanings

These names below are sorted by different meanings. The meaning is located at the top of each subsequent list. Each list is also sorted from Z-A.

Pearl

> **Lulu,** Origin: Teutonic, Arabic
> **Megan**, Origin: Greek, Irish
> **Margarita**, Origin: Spanish, Greek, Italian
> **Penina**, Origin: Hebrew
> **Magali,** Origin: Greek
> **Margaret,** Origin: Greek
> **Maille,** Origin: Celtic, Irish
> **Meg,** Origin: Celtic, English
> **Mairéad**, Origin: Irish
> **Marjorie,** Origin: Greek, English

Peace

- **Zell,** Origin: Hebrew
- **Yen,** Origin: Vietnamese
- **Winifred,** Origin: Celtic, German
- **Shiloh,** Origin: Hebrew
- **Shanti,** Origin: Sanskrit
- **Shalom**, Origin: Hebrew
- **Serenity,** Origin: English, Latin
- **Serena,** Origin: Latin
- **Selima,** Origin: Hebrew
- **Salomé,** Origin: Hebrew
- **Peace**, Origin: English
- **Paz,** Origin: Hebrew, Spanish
- **Pax,** Origin: Latin
- **Pacifica**, Origin: Spanish
- **Pace,** Origin: English
- **Noé,** Origin: Hebrew
- **Noah,** Origin: Hebrew
- **Noa**, Origin: Hebrew
- **Naima,** Origin: Arabic

- **Malu**, Origin: Hawaiian
- **Malia,** Origin: Hebrew, Hawaiian
- **Luba**, Origin: Polish
- **Lana,** Origin: Celtic, Old German, English
- **Jerusalem,** Origin: Hebrew
- **Irene,** Origin: Greek
- **Iraina,** Origin: Russian
- **Frieda,** Origin: Teutonic, German
- **Frida,** Origin: Teutonic, German
- **Frederica**, Origin: Teutonic, German
- **Fia**, Origin: Italian, Scottish
- **Dove**, Origin: English
- **Chesney**, Origin: French, English
- **Amandeep**, Origin: Sanskrit
- **Alana**, Origin: Celtic, Old German, Irish

Mother

- **Lavinia**, Origin: Latin
- **Danae,** Origin: Greek
- **Demetria,** Origin: Greek
- **Medora**, Origin: English, Greek
- **Imogen**, Origin: Celtic, English
- **Odilia**, Origin: English, Hebrew, German
- **Abra,** Origin: Hebrew

Love

- **Yaretzi**, Origin: Aztec, American
- **Xylophia,** Origin: Greek
- **Venus**, Origin: Greek, Latin
- **Thandie,** Origin: African
- **Tanith,** Origin: African, Phoenician
- **Taffy,** Origin: Welsh
- **Suki,** Origin: Japanese
- **Sherry**, Origin: Hebrew, English, French
- **Pleasant**, Origin: English
- **Phillipa,** Origin: Greek
- **Paris,** Origin: Greek, French
- **Pandora,** Origin: Greek
- **Nayeli**, Origin: American, Latin, Native American
- **Nahid,** Origin: Persian
- **Myrna,** Origin: Arabic, Celtic, Irish
- **Maite,** Origin: Spanish
- **Ludmilla,** Origin: Russian, Slavic
- **Lida,** Origin: Russian, Slavic
- **Leba**, Origin: Yiddish

- ➤ **Laramie,** Origin: French
- ➤ **Kyla**, Origin: Celtic, Scottish, Hebrew
- ➤ **Karissa,** Origin: Greek
- ➤ **Kalila,** Origin: Arabic
- ➤ **Heart**, Origin: English
- ➤ **Halia,** Origin: Greek, Hawaiian
- ➤ **Habiba**, Origin: Arabic
- ➤ **Gertrude**, Origin: Teutonic, German
- ➤ **Gael**, Origin: Celtic, English, Greek
- ➤ **Filippa**, Origin: Greek
- ➤ **Esmé,** Origin: French
- ➤ **Dodie**, Origin: Hebrew
- ➤ **Didi**, Origin: Hebrew
- ➤ **Derica,** Origin: Teutonic, German
- ➤ **Davida,** Origin: Hebrew
- ➤ **Cherish,** Origin: English
- ➤ **Cheri,** Origin: French
- ➤ **Cher**, Origin: French
- ➤ **Cerie**, Origin: Welsh
- ➤ **Ceridwen**, Origin: Welsh
- ➤ **Carissa**, Origin: French, Greek
- ➤ **Caris**, Origin: Welsh
- ➤ **Brisa**, Origin: Spanish
- ➤ **Aphrodite**, Origin: Greek

- **Amy**, Origin: French, Portuguese, Latin
- **Amoretta,** Origin: Latin
- **Amara**, Origin: Greek
- **Amanda**, Origin: Latin
- **Aimee,** Origin: French

Angel

- > **Zeraphina,** Origin: Hebrew
- > **Tang**i, Origin: American
- > **Seraphim**, Origin: Hebrew
- > **Serafina**, Origin: Spanish, Hebrew
- > **Heaven**, Origin: American, English
- > **Gina**, Origin: Greek, Italian
- > **Dangelo**, Origin: Italian, Greek
- > **D'Angela**, Origin: American
- > **Angie**, Origin: Greek, Latin
- > **Angelique**, Origin: French, Greek
- > **Angeline,** Origin: French, Latin, Russian
- > **Angelina**, Origin: Greek, Latin
- > **Angelica**, Origin: Latin, Greek
- > **Angela**, Origin: Greek, French, Mexican
- > **Angel**, Origin: Greek

Happy

- **Trixie,** Origin: English, Latin
- **Sharmila,** Origin: Hindi, Indian
- **Radhiya,** Origin: African, Swahili
- **Merry**, Origin: English
- **Keiko**, Origin: Japanese
- **Gaye**, Origin: English
- **Felicity**, Origin: Latin, English
- **Felicia,** Origin: Latin
- **Felice**, Origin: Italian, Latin
- **Desdemona**, Origin: Greek
- **Blythe**, Origin: English
- **Beatrix**, Origin: English, Latin
- **Beatrice**, Origin: Latin
- **Bea,** Origin: American, English
- **Alaia**, Origin: Arabic, Basque
- **Adamaris**, Origin: American
- **Ada**, Origin: Teutonic, Hebrew, English

Beautiful

- **Zaniah,** Origin: Arabic
- **Zaina,** Origin: Arabic
- **Yamilla,** Origin: Arabic
- **Yaffa**, Origin: Hebrew
- **Vashti,** Origin: Persian
- **Trixibelle**, Origin: American
- **Teagan**, Origin: Celtic, Irish, Welsh
- **Sohna**, Origin: Indian
- **Shifra**, Origin: Hebrew
- **Shayna,** Origin: Yiddish, Hebrew
- **Rupali,** Origin: Indian
- **Rosabelle**, Origin: French, Italian
- **Olathe,** Origin: Native American
- **Nefertiti**, Origin: Egyptian, Ancient Egyptian
- **Navit,** Origin: Hebrew
- **Mirabella,** Origin: Latin
- **Miki**, Origin: Japanese
- **Mika,** Origin: Japanese
- **Mieko,** Origin: Japanese
- **Maribel**, Origin: Spanish, Mexican, French
- **Lulabelle**, Origin: American

- **Kunani,** Origin: Hawaiian
- **Kimi,** Origin: Japanese
- **Kennis,** Origin: Gaelic
- **Kelis**, Origin: American
- **Kalidas**, Origin: Greek
- **Jamilla**, Origin: Arabic
- **Jaffa**, Origin: Hebrew
- **Ilona**, Origin: Greek, Hungarian
- **Hiraani**, Origin: Hawaiian
- **Hermosa**, Origin: Spanish
- **Gamila**, Origin: Arabic
- **Farrah,** Origin: English
- **Ella,** Origin: Spanish, English, Greek
- **Ella,** Origin: English
- **Eavan,** Origin: Celtic, Gaelic
- **Clarabell,** Origin: Latin
- **Christabel**, Origin: English, Latin
- **Calliope,** Origin: Greek
- **Callalily**, Origin: Greek
- **Calla,** Origin: Greek
- **Calista,** Origin: Greek
- **Belva,** Origin: Latin
- **Belle**, Origin: French
- **Bellamy,** Origin: French
- **Bella**, Origin: Hebrew, Latin

- **Belinda**, Origin: Latin, Spanish
- **Beila**, Origin: French, Spanish
- **Arabella**, Origin: English, Latin
- **Anwen,** Origin: Welsh
- **Annabella**, Origin: Latin, English
- **Anahi**, Origin: Persian, Spanish
- **Aloha**, Origin: Hawaiian
- **Alika**, Origin: Swahili

Princess

- **Zaria,** Origin: Russian, Latin, Hebrew
- **Zara,** Origin: Arabic, Hebrew
- **Zadie,** Origin: English
- **Tiana,** Origin: Greek, Latin
- **Tia**, Origin: Greek, Spanish
- **Suri**, Origin: Persian, Hebrew
- **Soraya**, Origin: Persian
- **Sarita**, Origin: Indian, Hebrew
- **Sariah,** Origin: Hebrew
- **Sari,** Origin: Arabic, Hebrew
- **Sarai,** Origin: Hebrew
- **Sarahi**, Origin: Hebrew
- **Sarah,** Origin: Hebrew
- **Sally**, Origin: Hebrew, English
- **Sadie,** Origin: Hebrew
- **Elmira**, Origin: Arabic
- **Damita**, Origin: Spanish
- **Amira**, Origin: Arabic, Hebrew

Chapter 5 – Thousands of Boy and Girl Names

The following is a list of both girl and boy names together with meaning and origin sorted from A-Z. Many of our readers requested that one list should not be sorted by gender so they could easily find the male or female counterpart of the name next to it. The innate meaning, spiritual connotation and origin can be found on the right side for most names. Best of luck, we sincerely hope that you will strike gold!

A

> **Aristotle,** Ari, Arias, Arie,

> **Acton**, Akton, Origin: Old English, Meaning: Oak-Tree Settlement, Agreeable

> **Allyson**, Origin: Old German, Meaning: Truthful, Holy

> **Alexxander**, Origin: Greek, Meaning: Defender of Mankind, Brave Protector

> **Antonia**, Antoinette,

- **Alecksander,** Alexandar,
- **Alexandra**, Aleksandra,
- **Agnes,**
- **Adeline**, Adalina, Adella,
- **Alexa,** Aleksa, Aleksia,
- **Alexandria**, Lexandra, Origin: Greek, Meaning: Defender of Mankind, Generous
- **Adreyan**, Adriaan,
- **Alllson**, Alicen, Alicyn,
- **Allan**, Alan, Origin: Irish, Meaning: Harmonious At One With Creation
- **Ashlynn**
- **Ashlen**, Ashlin, Ashling,
- **Ailina**, Origin: English, Meaning: Light Bearer, Messenger of Truth
- **Annika**, Origin: Czech, Meaning: Favor, Grace of God
- **Anthoney**, Anthonie,
- **Ariana**, Aeriana, Arianna,
- **Aubrey**, Aubray,
- **Adryon**, Origin: Greek, Meaning: Rich, Prosperous
- **Ashleigh,** Origin: Old English, Meaning: Of the Ash- Tree Meadow, Harmony

- ➤ **Albert**, Al, Alberto, Elbert, Origin: Old English, Meaning: Noble Brilliant
- ➤ **Allysa**, Origin: English, Meaning: Noble, Bold
- ➤ **Alim,** Aleem, Origin: Middle Eastern Meaning: Scholar Wise
- ➤ **Amanda**, Amandah,
- ➤ **Allegra,** Alegrea,
- ➤ **Audrey**, Audra, Audray,
- ➤ **Adriann**a, Adriana, Origin: Italian, Meaning: Dark Guarded of God
- ➤ **Aaron,** Origin: Danish, Meaning: Eagle, Perseverance
- ➤ **Atwell**, Attwell, Origin: English, Meaning: From the Well, Refreshing
- ➤ **Arman**d, Armando,
- ➤ **Asriel,**
- ➤ **Asreel**, Asreyel
- ➤ **Abrie**l, Abrielle, Origin: French, Meaning: Innocent Tenderhearted
- ➤ **Alice,** Alis, Allis, Alysse, Origin: Greek, Meaning: One of Integrity, Truthful
- ➤ **Alea**, Aleah, Aleea,
- ➤ **Adonijah**, Adonia,

- **Althea**, Origin: Greek, Meaning: Healer, Wholesome
- **Aiesha**, Aesha, Aisha,
- **Anni,**
- **Andrea**, Andee, Andi,
- **Alyssa**, (see Alisa)
- **Avery**, Averey, Averie, Origin: Middle Eastern, Meaning: Ruler Wise Counselor
- **Alisha**, Aleasha,
- **Alicia**, Alica, Alicea,
- **Ardon**, Ardan, Arden,
- **Aline**, Origin: Old German, Meaning: Noble, Righteous
- **Ali,** Origin: Swahili, Meaning: Exalted, Greatest
- **Augustine,** Origin: Latin, Meaning: Venerable, Exalted
- **Ashley**, Ashelee,
- **Anthony,** Anfernee,
- **Aron,** Arran, Arron, Origin: Hebrew, Meaning: Light Bringer Radiating, God's Light
- **Amadeus,**
- **Amos,** Origin: Hebrew, Meaning: Bearer of Burden, Compassionate
- **Alisa**, Alissa, Allissa,

- **Amelia**, Amaley, Amalia,
- **Amiran**, Ameiran
- **Aurel**, Aurele, Aurelio, Origin: Czech, Meaning: From Aurek, Reverent
- **Adriann,** Adianne,
- **Adrian**, Adreian,
- **Arni**, Arnie, Origin: Old German, Meaning: Strong as an Eagle, Brave
- **Atleigh,** Origin: English, Meaning: From the Meadow, Purchased
- **Alyx**, Allyx, Origin: Hungarian, Meaning: Defender of Mankind Benefactor
- **Adaya**, Origin: Hebrew, Meaning: God's Jewel, Valuable
- **Ardelle**, Ardella, Origin: Latin, Meaning: Eager, Spirit of Praise
- **Adam**, Origin: Hebrew, Meaning: Formed of Earth, In God's Image
- **Alan**, Al, Allan, Alen
- **Amery**, Aimery, Ameri,
- **Ani**, Origin: Hawaiian, Meaning: Beautiful, Lovely in Spirit,
- **Ann,** Anne, Annette,

- **Ava,** Origin: Hebrew, Meaning: From the Palace, Blessed
- **Antonio**, Antonius, Origin: Italian, Meaning: Priceless, Righteous
- **Addison,**
- **Adelyn**, Origin: Hebrew, Meaning: Honor, Courageous
- **Ace**, Origin: Latin, Meaning: Unity One With the Father
- **Angelea**,
- **Aldis,** Origin: Anglo-Saxon, Meaning: Wise Protector, Guided of God
- **Alonzo,**
- **Almeira,** Origin: Middle Eastern, Meaning: Princess, Fulfillment of Truth
- **Aurora**, Aurore, Origin: Latin, Meaning: Dawn, Mouthpiece of God
- **Adriel**, Origin: Hebrew, Meaning: Member of Gods Flock, Nurtured of God
- **Anson,** Origin: Old German, Meaning: Divine, Partaker in Glory
- **Ariel**, Aerial, Aeriell,
- **Audie**, Origin: Old English, Meaning: Property Guardian, Strong of Heart

- **Allyster,** Origin: Scottish, Meaning: Defender, Courage
- **Alfonso**, Alfonzo,
- **Asa**, Origin: Hebrew, Meaning: Healer, Healer of the Mind
- **Adria**, Origin: Latin, Meaning: Love of Life, Filled With Life
- **Abram**, Origin: Hebrew, Meaning: Father of Nations, Founder
- **Augustus**, August,
- **Antoine**, Antony, (see
- **Amie**, Ammy, Origin: Latin, Meaning: Beloved, Serene Spirit
- **Angi**, Origin: Greek, Meaning: Angel/Messenger, Bringer of Glad Tidings
- **Allegrea**, Origin: Latin, Meaning: Cheerful, Eager to Live
- **Alejandro**, Alejandra,
- **Adiel**, Addiel, Addielle, Hebrew, Meaning: Ornament of God, Lovely
- **Annabell**, Origin: Latin, Meaning: Graceful, Beloved
- **Ariyel**,
- **Andrew,**

- **Alexandros**, Alexius,
- **Alianna**, Origin: Scottish, Meaning: Bearer of Light, Ambassador of Truth
- **Arric,** Origin: Old German, Meaning: Joyful, Spirit of Joy
- **Avis,** Avia, Aviana, Origin: Latin, Meaning: Refuge, Place of Freedom
- **Allen,** Origin: Irish, Meaning: Harmonious At One With Creation
- **Adisson,** Origin: Old English, Meaning: Son of Adam In God's Image
- **Aleck**, Aleksandar,
- **Adrien**, Adriene, Origin: Greek, Meaning: Confident Faith in God
- **Alexander**, Alax, Alec,
- **Amada,** Amadea,
- **Alvyn,** Origin: German, Meaning: Friend of All, Sincere
- **Aileen**, Ailean, Ailene,
- **Athena**, Athina, Origin: Greek, Meaning: Wise Mind of God
- **Amber**, Ambur, (see also
- **Austyn**, Origin: Latin, Meaning: Renowned, Guided of God
- **Alvin**, Al, Alvan, Alven,

- **Angie,** Angelena,
- **Anna**, Gracious, Meaning: Full of Grace
- **Alva**, (see also Elva), Latin, Meaning: Brightness, Alive
- **Adrienne**, Adriane,
- **Antonette**, Antonia, Origin: Russian, Meaning: Favor of God, Peace
- **Arnold,** Arne, Arney,
- **Ashby**, Origin: English, Meaning: From the Ash-Tree Farm, Fear of God
- **Ashlyn**, Ashlyne,
- **Ashton**, Origin: English, Meaning: From the Ash-Tree Farm, Supplicant
- **Ashlea,**
- **Alvis**, (see also Elvis) Scandinavian, Meaning: All-Knowing Conqueror
- **Allastair**, Allaster, Allastir,
- **Asriel**, Origin: Hebrew, Meaning: God Helped, Delivered
- **Amy,** Aimee, Aimey,
- **Andrei**, Andres, Andy,
- **Allie**, Anglo-Saxon, Meaning: Brilliant Illuminated
- **Alexis,** Aleksei, Aleksey,

- **Adora**, Adoree, Latin, Meaning: Beloved, Gift of God
- **Aurielle,** Origin: Latin, Meaning: Golden, Sealed
- **Adrien**, Adrion, Adryan,
- **Adina**, Origin: Hebrew, Meaning: Adorned, Clothed With Praise
- **Axel**,
- **Abiel**, Abielle, Origin: Hebrew, Meaning: Child of God, Heir of the Kingdom
- **Arial,** Ariale, Arielle,
- **Anton,** Origin: Slavic, Meaning: One of Value, Eloquent
- **Adia**, Origin: African, Meaning: Gift, Gift of Glory
- **Austin**, Austan, Austen,
- **Aimie**, Aimmie, Aimy,
- **Angeline**,
- **Agnessa**, Origin: Greek, Meaning: Pure, Innocent
- **Arlene,** Arlana, Arleen,
- **Aladdin,** Origin: Middle Eastern, Meaning: Pinnacle of Faith, Righteous
- **Alex**, Alexia, Allex, Allix,

- **Angelo**, Origin: Italian, Meaning: Angel/Messenger, Bringer of Glad Tidings
- **Amadeo**, Origin: Latin, Meaning: Lover of God, Obedient
- **Audrianna**, Origin: Old English, Meaning: Noble Strength, Overcomer of Many Difficulties
- **Andreia**, Andreya, Andria, Origin: Greek, Meaning: Womanly Filled With Grace
- **Alpha**, Origin: Phoenician, Meaning: Ox, Restful
- **Angela**, Angee, Angel,
- **Adelle**, Adelynn, Origin: Old German, Meaning: Noble, Under God's Guidance
- **Asheleigh**, Asheley,
- **Amira,** Origin: Hebrew, Meaning: Speech, Unhidden
- **Aleksi**, Alexes, Alexis,
- **Angeliana**, Angelina,
- **Asha**, Origin: Middle Eastern, Meaning: Vitality, Humble Strength
- **Ada**, Adah, Adalee, Aida, Origin: Hebrew, Meaning: Ornament, One Who Adorns
- **Azarel,**

B

- **Boyde**, Boid, Origin: Scottis, Meaning: Golden-Haired, Quiet, Spirit
- **Bali**, Baylee, Bayley,
- **Brant**, Brandt, Brannt,
- **Bruce**, Bruse, Origin: Scottish, Meaning: From the Woods, Dignity
- **Bowen**, Bowie, Origin: Gaelic, Meaning: Small, Victorious
- **Brodric**, Broadrick
- **Barclay**, Barkley,
- **Bessy**, Origin: English, Meaning: Oath of God, Loyal
- **Beatrice**, Bea, Beatricia,
- **Brodie**, Brodee, Brodey,
- **Becky**, Becca, Becka,
- **Briana**, Briannah,
- **Bryant**, Bryen, Bryent,
- **Boris**, Boriss, Borris, Origin: Slavic, Meaning: Warrior, Trusting

- **Boone**, Boon, Boonie, Origin: French, Meaning: Good, Obedient
- **Bob**, (see Robert)
- **Brandin**, Brandyn,
- **Brennon**, Origin: Irish, Meaning: Little Raven, Gift of God
- **Benson,** Bensen, Origin: English, Meaning: Son of Ben, Honor of God
- **Brendin**, Brendon,
- **Brenndan**, Origin: Irish, Meaning: Stinking Hair, Devout
- **Baylie**, Origin: Old French, Meaning: Stewardship, Protector
- **Brannan**, Brannon, Origin: Old English, Meaning: From the Flaming, Hill Fervent
- **Benyamin**, Origin: Hebrew, Meaning: Son of My Right Hand, Mighty
- **Brindley**, Brinlee, Brinly,
- **Bertram**, Bartram, Bert, Origin: Old English, Meaning: Brilliant, Magnificent
- **Bonnie**, Bonita, Bonne,
- **Baden**, Origin: Hebrew, Meaning: Son of Judgment, Encourager

- **Brianna**, Origin: Celtic, Meaning: Strong, Dependent
- **Blair**, Blaire, Origin: Irish, Meaning: Field Worker, Diligent
- **Bane**, Bayne
- **Barney**, Barnie, Origin: Hebrew, Meaning: Son of Exhortation, Praise to God
- **Brynley**, Origin: Old English, Meaning: Burnt Wood, Sacrifice
- **Britny**, Brityn, Brittain,
- **Bain**, Baine
- **Braden**, Bradan, Bradin,
- **Braxton**, Braxtun, Origin: Old English, Meaning: From Brock's Town Faithful
- **Brantley**, Origin: Czech, Meaning: Proud, Focused
- **Bernice**, Berenice, Berni,
- **Brandi**, Brandie, Origin: Middle Dutch, Meaning: Distilled Wine, Filled With Joy
- **Bane,** Origin: Gaelic, Meaning: Fair, Cleansed
- **Brenda**, Brendie, Origin: Old Norse, Meaning: Sword, Glory of God
- **Brian**, Briant, Brien,
- **Britaney**, Britani,

- **Bannie**, Origin: Hebrew, Meaning: Built, Honorable
- **Beldon,** Belden, Origin: Old English, Meaning: From the Beautiful Valley, Sanctified
- **Britanny,** Britlee, Britley,
- **Belinda**, Belynda, Origin: Spanish, Meaning: Lovely, Beauty of Soul
- **Barbara,** Barb, Barbe,
- **Brendan**, Brenden,
- **Belle,** Bell, Bellina, Origin: French, Meaning: Beautiful, Blessed
- **Bradlee**, Origin: Old English, Meaning: From the Broad, Meadow Joyful
- **Bryan**, see Brian
- **Bradon**, Origin: English, Meaning: From the Broad, Clearing Redeemed
- **Bradon**, Braedon,
- **Bennie,** Benny,
- **Bobbie**, Bobbi, Origin: American, Meaning: Foreigner, Stranger
- **Britney**, Britni, Britnie,
- **Bernadette,** Bernadine, Origin: French, Meaning: Courageous, Valiant
- **Bronson,** Bronnson,

- **Bradin,** Braeden,
- **Blade**, Blayde, Origin: Middle English, Meaning: Knife, Weapon
- **Bradford,** Brad,
- **Beth Ann**, Bethann, BethAnn,
- **Brenton**, Brendt, Brent,
- **Bernie**, Birnee, Birney,
- **Brit**, Brita, Britt, Britte, Origin: Swedish, Mcaning: Strong, Prayerful
- **Breanne**, Breann, BreAnn,
- **Bridgett**, Bridgette,
- **Boyce**, Boice, Boise,
- **Bevin**, Bevin, Origin: Welsh, Meaning: Son of the Young Warrior Youthful
- **Bessie**, Bess, Bessi,
- **Bre-Anne**, Breeann,
- **Brittanee**, Brittaney,
- **Brok**, Broque, Origin: Old English, Meaning: Badger, Full of Praise
- **Bodin,** Origin: French, Meaning: Messenger/Herald, Ready for Service
- **Brennan**, Brennen,
- **Bonni**, Bonnita, Bonny, Origin: French, Meaning: Beautiful, Pure in Heart
- **Birdie,** (See Roberta)

- **Bianca,** Biancha, Bionca,
- **Bailey**, Bailee, Bailie,
- **Benjamin**, Ben,
- **Branddon**, Branden,
- **Brodi**, Origin: Irish, Meaning: Canal Builder, God Is My Foundation
- **Bradley**, Brad, Bradd,
- **Baker**, see Baxter
- **Barry**, Barrey, Bary, Origin: Irish, Meaning: Marksman, Strong
- **Brook**, Brooke, Brooks,
- **Bryce**, Brice, Origin: Welsh, Meaning: Responsive Ambitious
- **Bethani**, Bethanie,
- **Braden,** Origin: English, Meaning: From the Hill, Called of God
- **Breck**, Brec, Brek, Brekk Origin: Irish, Meaning: Freckled Approved
- **Brittany**, Britain, Britane,
- **Brandy**, Brandee,
- **Burton,** Berton, Burt, Origin: Middle English, Meaning: From the Fortified Town Amply, Supplied
- **Briele,** Brielle, Brieon,

- **Bambi**, Bambee, Bambie, Origin: Italian, Meaning: Child, Innocent
- **Brock**, Broc, Brocke,
- **Brennah**, Brennaugh,
- **Betsie,** Origin: English, Meaning: Oath of God, Confirmed
- **Britlyn**, Britynn, Britnee,
- **Betty**, Bett, Bette, Bette,
- **Blake,** Blakelee,
- **Bernard**, Barnard,
- **Baxter**, Baker, Origin: Middle English, Meaning: Provider Industrious
- **Betti**, Bettie, Origin: English, Meaning: Oath of God, Reverent
- **Brina**, Breena, Breina,
- **Bill,** (see William)
- **Brandon**, Brandan,
- **Broderick**, Broderic,
- **Burney**, Origin: Old German, Meaning: Brave as a Bear, Wise
- **Breanna**, Breeana,
- **Blaine**, Blain, Blane,
- **Brady**, Origin: Scandinavian, Meaning: Glacier, Immovable
- **Brady**, Bradey

- **Bruno**, Origin: Old German, Meaning: Brown, Rich in God's Grace
- **Blaise**, Blaize, Blayze,
- **Bridget**, Bridgete,
- **Bennet**, Bennett, Origin: English, Meaning: Blessed Walks With God
- **Balin**, Baylin

C

- **Candria**, Kandra, Origin: Latin, Meaning: Incandescent, Reflection of Christ
- **Cort**, see Cortney
- **Clark**, Clarke, Origin: Old French, Meaning: Scholar, Enlightened Spirit
- **Caterina**, see Katerina
- **Callaghan**, Origin: Irish, Meaning: Saint, Faithful
- **Clarissa**, Claresa,
- **Crandell**, Crandall, Origin: English, Meaning: From the Valley, Freedom
- **Carter**, Cartar, Origin: Old English, Meaning: Driver of a Cart, Privileged
- **Clyff**, Origin: Old English, Meaning: From the River's Heights, Vigilant
- **Carli**, Carlie, Karlee,
- **Caron**, Carron, Carrone, Origin: Welsh, Meaning: Loving, Witness
- **Chrystin**, Cristan, Cristen,

- **Coniah**, Coniyah, Origin: Hebrew, Meaning: God-Appointed, Destined
- **Caysee**, Caysey, Caysie,
- **Candace**, Candice,
- **Cameron**, Cam,
- **Christen**, Christyn,
- **Casimir**, Cachie, Cash,
- **Carynn**, (see also Karen,
- **Cassidy**, Cass, Cassady,
- **Cheryl**, Chereen,
- **Charis**, Charisa,
- **Cristofer**, Cristopher,
- **Chloe**, Chloee, Cloe,
- **Christine**, Christeen,
- **Clarrisa**, Clarissa,
- **Carlana**, Caraena,
- **Candra**, Candrea,
- **Christian**, Christiaan,
- **Chriss**, Christepher,
- **Codi**, Codie, Kodee,
- **Carianne,** Carena
- **Chickara**, Chickarra,
- **Carliana**, Karleena,

- **Cissy**, Cissee, Origin: American, Meaning: Blind, Discerning
- **Charlene**, Charline,
- **Carolyn**, Carrolin,
- **Carys**, Caris, Carris,
- **Charles**, Charle,
- **Colby**, Colbey, Colbi,
- **Carmon**, Karman,
- **Concieta**, Origin: Italian, Meaning: Pure, Undefiled
- **Christiane**, Christiann,
- **Chalise**, Chalissa,
- **Colin,** Colan, Colen,
- **Cody**, Codee, Codey,
- **Charlton,** Charleton,
- **Connor**, Conner,
- **Canute**, see Knute
- **Carol,** Carel, Carole,
- **Charese**, Charice,
- **Cozbie,** Cozby, Origin: Canaanite, Meaning: Deceiver, Loving
- **Chrystan**, Chrysten,
- **Chrisie,** Chrissey,
- **Clarisa,** Clarisse,
- **Caecilia,** Cece, Cecelia,

- **Cannen,** Canning, Canon
- **Clarance,** Clarrance,
- **Charlotte**, Charlette,
- **Canaan**, Caenan,
- **Cyprianne**, Origin: Greek, Meaning: From Cyprus, Bold Witness
- **Conroy**, Conroye, Origin: Irish, Meaning: Wise Strong Leader
- **Carrol**, Carrell, Caroll,
- **Charley**, Charlic, Origin: English, Meaning: Manly, Valiant
- **Chrystal**, Chrystel,
- **Charissa**, Charesa,
- **Cecilea**, Cecillia, CeeCee, Origin: Latin, Meaning: Blind Of the Spirit
- **Carlina**, Carleena,
- **Cindy,** see Cythia
- **Carmelia**, Carmella,
- **Callee**, Calleigh, Calli,
- **Cyrus,** Cy, Cyris, Origin: Persian, Meaning: Sun Spiritual Enlightenment
- **Christianna**, Christinna,
- **Cyril**, Cyrill, Cyrille, Origin: Greek, Meaning: Lordly, Great Spiritual Potential

- **Corwin**, Corwyn, Origin: Latin, Meaning: Heart's Delight, Brilliant Countenance
- **Carla**, Carlia, Karla,
- **Claudius**, Claude,
- **Conny,** Konnie, Origin: English, Meaning: Consistent, Unwavering
- **Carroll** (see also Carol), Origin: Gaelic, Meaning: Champion, Steadfast
- **Chrysti**, Chrystle,
- **Casondra**, Cassaundra,
- **Chiara**, Chiarah, Origin: Italian, Meaning: Clear, Sealed
- **Challis**, Challisse,
- **Clyde**, Clide, Origin: Welsh, Meaning: Loving, Rewarded
- **Candi,** Candy, Candyce,
- **Carlan**, Carlen, Carlii,
- **Christene**, Chrystine,
- **Claudell**, Claudio, Origin: Latin, Meaning: Lame Loved
- **Cristin** (see also Kristen), Origin: English, Meaning: Follower of Christ, Obedient
- **Clarence**, Clare,
- **Chanah**, Chana, Channa, Origin: Hebrew, Meaning: Favor of God, Prayerful

- ➤ **Crosby**, Crosbie, Origin: Scandinavian, Meaning: Shrine of the Cross, Reminder of Christ
- ➤ **Charleen**, Charlaine,
- ➤ **Cassandra**, Casandera,
- ➤ **Cedrik**, Origin: English, Meaning: Battle Chieftain. Courageous Defender
- ➤ **Cambria**, Camberlee,
- ➤ **Caillin,** Calan, Calin,
- ➤ **Channing**, Chane,
- ➤ **Cristina**, Cristiona,
- ➤ **Cathy**, Cathee, Cathey,
- ➤ **Cortez**, Courtez, Origin: Spanish, Meaning: Conqueror, Valiant
- ➤ **Caitlynn,** Catlin (see also
- ➤ **Carmielle,** Carmiya,
- ➤ **Crayton,** Origin: English, Meaning: From the Rocky Place, Humble Spirit
- ➤ **Coley**, Colee, Colee,
- ➤ **Carroline**
- ➤ **Chantrea**, Chantria, Origin: Cambodian, Meaning: Moonbeam, Symbol
- ➤ **Carmen,** Carmain,

- **Chiko,** Chikora, Origin: Japanese, Meaning: Pledge, Promise
- **Cindie**, Cindy, Cynda,
- **Camden**, Camdan, Origin: Old English, Meaning: From the Winding, Valley Freedom
- **Collier**, Collyer, Origin: Welsh, Meaning: Merchant or Miner, Guided of God
- **Carlissa**, Carlisa,
- **Carlos**, Carlo, Karlo,
- **Crystall**, Crystallin,
- **Carrie**, Carree, Carri,
- **Calvin,** Cal, Origin: Latin, Meaning: Bald, Favored
- **Cozbi,** Cosbey, Cosbie,
- **Campbell**, Cambell, Origin: French, Meaning: Beautiful Field, Consistent
- **Camille,** Camila, Camill,
- **Chalmers**, Chalmer,
- **Claus**, see Klaus
- **Clarinda,** Clarita, Origin: French, Meaning: Brilliant, Shining Light
- **Cory**, see Corey
- **Calista**, Calista, Calysta,
- **Consuela**, Konsuela, Origin: Spanish, Meaning: Consoling Friend, Compassionate

- **Catalina**, Catalena,
- **Carolee**, Carolea,
- **Christie**, Christy, Chrys,
- **Chalina,** Chaeena,
- **Cannon**, Cannan,
- **Cashmere,** Cashmir,
- **Casey**, Cacey, Cacy,
- **Caryn**, Caren, Carin,
- **Cammy** (see also Kami), Origin: French, Meaning: Ceremonial Attendant, Helper
- **Cortney**, Cortni, Cortnie,
- **Cynthia**, Cindee, Cindi,
- **Cameran,** Camren,
- **Calhoun,** Origin: Scottish, Meaning: Strong Warrior, Great in Spirit
- **Colbert**, Culbert, Origin: English, Meaning: Brilliant Seafarer Anchored in God
- **Conciana**, Concianna,
- **Cobi**, Cobie, Kobe,
- **Cypriana,** Cyprianna,
- **Caitlin,** Caitlan, Caitland,
- **Charity**, Chaitee, Chariti, Origin: English, Meaning: Benevolent, Compassionate
- **Cortne,** Cortnee,

- **Coby**, Cobe, Cobey,
- **Carlotta**, Karlotta, Origin: Italian, Meaning: Womanly Godly Heroine
- **Cooper**, Courper, Origin: English, Meaning: Barrel Maker, Servant
- **Carlin**, Karilynn, Karolyn, Origin: French, Meaning: Womanly, Filled With Praise
- **Christianos**, Christion,
- **Christopher,** Chris,,
- **Carry** (see also Carey,
- **Cary**, Caree, Carree,
- **Creed**, Creedon, Origin: Latin, Meaning: Belief, Power in Faith
- **Cami,** Cammi, Cammie,
- **Coy**, Coi, Koy, Origin: English, Meaning: From the Woods, Focused
- **Clancy**, Clancey, Origin: Irish, Meaning: Red-Haired Fighter, Christlike
- **Caroleigh,** Origin: American, Meaning: Little Beloved, Just
- **Clay**, Clae, Origin: English, Meaning: Malleable Earth, Adaptable
- **Christena,** Christiana,
- **Cady**, Cadee, Cadey,
- **Corttney,** Court,

- **Caroline**, Caralin,
- **Carson**, Carrson, Origin: English, Meaning: Diligent, Loyal
- **Cyndie**, Cyndy, Origin: Greek, Meaning: Moon Celestial Light
- **Chara**, Charah, Origin: Hispanic, Meaning: Rose, Joy
- **Claire**, Clair, Clara,
- **Chapman**, Chapmann, Origin: English, Meaning: Merchant, Wise
- **Case**, Casie, Casy,
- **Cara**, Caragh, Carah,
- **Cristian**, Cristiano,
- **Charlanna**, Charlena,
- **Carmela**, Carmalla,
- **Clayborne**, Claeborne, Origin: Middle English, Meaning: From the Clay Brook Molded by God
- **Cedric**, Cedrec, Cedric,
- **Caraline**, Carolin,
- **Chantha**, Chantra
- **Carita**, Caritta, Karita,
- **Clayton,** Clayten, Origin: Old English, Meaning: From the Clay Estate Molded by God

- **Caryss**, (see also Karis), Origin: Welsh, Meaning: Loving, Respectful
- **Cartrina,** see Katrina
- **Cowan**, Cowey, Origin: Irish, Meaning: From the Hillside, Generous
- **Celena**, see Selena
- **Clarrence**, Origin: Latin, Meaning: Victorious, Pure
- **Clemens**, Clement,
- **Cecil**, Cecile, Cecill Latin, Meaning: Blind Illuminated
- **Camron**, Kam, Kameron,
- **Conrad**, Conrade,
- **Channelle,** Channel,
- **Christen**, Christian,
- **Collette**, Kolette, Kollette
- **Casper**, Caspar, Origin: Persian, Meaning: Treasure, Watchful
- **Cari**, Kari, Origin: English, Meaning: Beloved, Redeemed
- **Courtney**, Cort, Cortnay,
- **Carissa,**
- **Chandler**, Chandan,
- **Camilla**, Cammille,

- **Carney,** Karney, Origin: Irish, Meaning: Victorious Preserved
- **Chandelle**, Chandal,
- **Charise**, Cher, Cherice,
- **Chistina**, Christeena,
- **Cherie**, Cheri, Cherie
- **Chester,** Ches, Cheston,
- **Criston**, Khristian, Kristar,
- **Camelia**, Camella,
- **Carmellina,** Carmelita, Origin: Italian, Meaning: Garden, Natured of God
- **Curtis,** Curt, Curtiss,
- **Carl**, Carel, Carle, Carlis,
- **Chesney,** Chesnie, Origin: Slavic, Meaning: Peaceful Regal, Servant
- **Craig**, Cregg, Crieg,
- **Coco**, Cocco, Coccoa
- **Casandra**, Casandria,
- **Corynn**, Origin: English, Meaning: Little, One Trusting
- **Cosby**, Coz, Cozbee,
- **Cato**, Caton (see also
- **Callie**, Caleigh, Cali,

- ➤ **Chaning**, Origin: English, Meaning: Wise, Obedient
- ➤ **Charelle**, Charil, Charyl,
- ➤ **Chalsey**, Origin: French, Meaning: Goblet, Cheerful
- ➤ **Caley**, Caylee, Cayley,
- ➤ **Carey**, Caray, Carrey
- ➤ **Coyle**, Coyel, Origin: Irish, Meaning: Courageous Leader, God's Warrior
- ➤ **Cecilia**, Cacelia,

D

- **Dean**, Deane, Dene, Origin: Old English, Meaning: Valley, Prosperous
- **Darnelle,** Darnall,
- **Danelle**, Origin: French, Meaning: God Is My Judge, Perceptive
- **Deanna**, Deana, Deann,
- **Doris**, Dorice, Dorise,
- **Dwayne**, DeWayne,
- **Delaiah**, Dalaiah, Origin: Hebrew, Meaning: God Is the Deliverer, Redeemed
- **Dayna**, Daynah, Origin: Scandinavian, Meaning: Bright as Day, Obedient
- **Doriann,** Dorianna,
- **Dejuan**, see Dejuan
- **Doyle**, Doyal, Origin: Irish, Meaning: Dark Stranger, Guided by the Spirit
- **Davine**, Davinia, Davira,
- **Daythan**, Daython, Origin: Hebrew, Meaning: Belonging to the Law, Redeemed

- **Deborrah**, Debra, Origin: Hebrew, Meaning: Honey Bee, New Era of Leadership
- **Demetrius**, Origin: Russian, Meaning: Immeasurable, Gracious
- **Dennzel**, Denzell, Denzil, Origin: English, Meaning: From Cornwall,
- **Darrick**, Darrik, Dereck,
- **Delano**, Dellano, Origin: French, Meaning: Nut Tree, Anchored
- **Darcie,** Darcy, Darsey,
- **Danae**, Danay, Dannae
- **Darby**, Darbey, Darbi,
- **Deimas**, Origin: Greek, Meaning: Ruler of People, Powerful
- **Deja,** Daija, Daja, Origin: French, Meaning: Before, Compassionate
- **Darrielle**, Origin: French, Meaning: Little Darling, Cherished
- **Dannon**, Danaan,
- **Dane,** Daine, Dayne,
- **Darryl**, Darryll, Daryl,
- **Dylana**, Dylanna, Origin: Welsh, Meaning: From the Sea, Devoted
- **Damarys**, Demaras,
- **Donald**, Don, Donn,

- **Davon,** Origin: English, Meaning: From Devonshire, Obedient
- **Donata,** Donatta, Origin: Latin, Meaning: Gift of God, Contemplative
- **Demario**, Origin: Italian, Meaning: Son of a Warrior, Seed of a Righteous Soldier
- **Drew**, Drewe, Dru, Drue, Origin: Welsh, Meaning: Wise, Esteemed
- **Demaris**, Demarius, Origin: Greek, Meaning: Gentle, Forgiven
- **Duston,** Dusty, Dustyn, Origin: German, Meaning: Valiant Warrior, Brave
- **Danyel**, Danyele,
- **Deandria**, Deanndra,
- **Denham**, Denhem, Origin: English, Meaning: From the Valley Village, One of Integrity
- **Dedrick,** Detrick, Didrik,
- **Durant**, Durand,
- **Debora,** Debora,
- **Dawson**, Dawsen, Origin: English, Meaning: Son of the Beloved, Victorious
- **Delsie**, Delcee, Delsee, Origin: English, Meaning: Oath of God, Promise
- **Danica**, Daneeka,

- ➢ **Dimitrios**, Dimitrius,
- ➢ **Deonna,** Deonne, Dione,
- ➢ **Dimitri**, Origin: Greek, Meaning: Lover of the Earth, Fruitful Increase
- ➢ **Demetri,** Dimitrie, Dmitri,
- ➢ **Dena,** Deena, Origin: Native American, Meaning: From the Valley, Peaceful
- ➢ **Dale**, Dayle, Origin: Old English, Meaning: From Valley, Peaceful
- ➢ **Desiree**, Desarae,
- ➢ **Deandra**, Deandrea,
- ➢ **Dillon,** Dillan, Dillen,
- ➢ **Delainey**, Delanny,
- ➢ **Dandrae,** Dandray,
- ➢ **Darin**, Darran, Darrian,
- ➢ **Dillin** (see also Dylan), Irish, Meaning: Faithful, Steadfast in Christ
- ➢ **Diedrick**, Origin: German, Meaning: Ruler of the People, Respected
- ➢ **Dyana**, Dyane, Dyann,
- ➢ **Deacon**, Deke, Diakonos, Origin: Greek, Meaning: One Who Serves, Honored
- ➢ **Dorothy**, Dottie, Dotti,
- ➢ **Dexter**, Dextor, Origin: Latin, Meaning: Skilled in Workmanship, Industrious

- **Danielle**, Danialle,
- **Dejuan**, Dewaun, Dijuan,
- **Darias**, Darien, Darion, Origin: Persian, Meaning: Prosperous Preserved
- **Dyanna**, Dyanne, Origin: Latin, Meaning: Divine, Glorious
- **Deanne**, Deeann,
- **Drisana,** Drisanna, Origin: Sanskrit, Meaning: Daughter of the Sun, Loyal
- **Deitra**, Deetra, Detria, Origin: Greek, Meaning: Abundant, Refreshed
- **Daniella**, Dannielle,
- **Delia**, Dehlia, Deleah,
- **Daniel**, Dan, Daniyel,
- **Diego,** Diaz, Origin: Spanish, Meaning: Supplanter, Wise
- **Daron,** Darren, Origin: Welsh, Meaning: Freedom, Spirit-Filled
- **Darynn,** Darynne,
- **Dayana**, Dayahna, Origin: Middle Eastern, Meaning: Divine, Warrior
- **Damica**, Damika,
- **Dustin,** Dustan, Dusten,

- **Diamonte**, Origin: Latin, Meaning: Precious Gem, Carefully Guarded
- **Daaina,** Dalina, Origin: German, Meaning: Noble Protector, Example
- **Deon,** Deion, Deone,
- **Damien,** Damion,
- **Dynah,** Origin: Hebrew, Meaning: God Has Vindicated, Righteous
- **Danell**, Dannell
- **Dagan,** Dagon, Origin: Hebrew, Meaning: Grain, Wise
- **D'Juan**, Dujuan, Origin: American, Meaning: God Is Gracious, Promise
- **David**, Dave, Daved,
- **Darral**, Darrel, Darril,
- **Dawn,** Dawnan, Dawna,
- **Dalayna**, Dalena, Dalina,
- **Darren**, Darius, Deron, Origin: English, Meaning: Rocky Hill, Obedient
- **Damonn**, Daymon, Origin: Greek, Meaning: Loyal, Walks With God
- **Devon**, Devonlee,
- **Demas,** Deemas,
- **Dorien,** Dorion, Dorrian,
- **Daveena,** Davi, Daviana,

- **Dorcas,** Origin: Greek, Meaning: Filled With Grace, Heir
- **Dajuan**, Dawan, Dawon,
- **Daniah**, Danie, Danni,
- **Dezmond,** Origin: Irish, Meaning: Youthful, Refreshing
- **Della,** Dellie, Origin: Old German, Meaning: Noble Maiden, Excellent Virtue
- **Dacian**, Dacien, Origin: Latin, Meaning: Southerner, Divine Perspective
- **Daman**, Damen,
- **Dante**, Dauntay,
- **Demetreus,**
- **Damara**, Damarrah, Origin: Czech, Meaning: Glory of the Day Promised Result
- **Daevon**, Davohn, Davon,
- **Davis**, Davidson, Davies,
- **Delores**, Deloria, Deloris,
- **Dewey,** Dewie, Origin: Welsh, Meaning: Prized, Prosperous
- **Domenico,** Domenick,
- **Dylon** (see also Dillon), Origin: Welsh, Meaning: From the Sea, Resolute Courage

- ➤ **Dalton**, Dalten, Origin: Old English, Meaning: From the Valley Town, Filled With Peace
- ➤ **Danya**, Danyah, Donya
- ➤ **Danny**, Donyel, Donyell, Origin: Hebrew, Meaning: God Is My Judge, Discerning
- ➤ **Danette**, Danett, Origin: American, Meaning: God Is My Judge, Perceptive
- ➤ **Denice**, Deniece,
- ➤ **Diana**, Daiana, Daianna,
- ➤ **Dimitri**, Demitre,
- ➤ **Dametra,** Origin: Spanish, Meaning: Noble Lady, Gracious Spirit
- ➤ **Dennise**, Origin: French, Meaning: Favored, Reborn
- ➤ **Darwin**, Darwyn, Origin: Old English, Meaning: Beloved, Treasured
- ➤ **Dierdre**, Origin: Irish, Meaning: Wanderer, Seeker of Righteousness and Truth
- ➤ **Devoney**, Devony, Origin: Gaelic, Meaning: Dark-Haired, Sacrifice
- ➤ **Dacia,** Dacia, Origin: Latin, Meaning: Southerner, Divine, Perspective
- ➤ **Dakota,** Dakotah, Origin: Sioux, Meaning: Friend, Sincere
- ➤ **Deena,** see Dena

- **Duncan,** Duncon, Origin: Scottish, Meaning: Steadfast Warrior, Strong in Faith
- **Danya,** Origin: Hebrew, Meaning: God Is My Judge, Intuitive
- **Desmon**, Desmund,
- **Dominika**, Origin: Latin, Meaning: Belonging to the Lord, Consecrated
- **Danen**, Danon, Origin: American, Meaning: God Is My Judge, Preserved
- **Daycee**, Daycic, Origin: Gaelic, Meaning: Southerner, Friend of Christ
- **Dwight**, Dwieght, Origin: English, Meaning: Fair, Diligent Leader
- **Daya**, Daeya, Daia, Origin: Hebrew, Meaning: Bird, Secure
- **Denton**, Dentin, Origin: English, Meaning: From a Happy Home, Trusting Spirit
- **Dolores,** Origin: Spanish, Meaning: Sorrowful, Compassionate
- **Dorothea**, Dorothee,
- **Dino,** Deeno, Origin: German, Meaning: Little Sword, Covenant
- **Dixon,** Dickson, Origin: English, Meaning: Son of the Ruler, Youthful Courage

- **Darlene**, Darla, Darleen,
- **Dhane,** Origin: Old English, Meaning: Trickling, Stream Blessed
- **Deirdre**, Dedra, Deedra,
- **Dagana**, Dagania,
- **Dericka**, Derrica, Derrika, Origin: German, Meaning: Ruler of the People, Gifted
- **Davin,** Daevin, Daevon,
- **Devin**, Devan, Deven,
- **Demetreaus**, Demetrias,
- **Dick**, Dic, Dickenson,
- **Derika**, Dereka, Derica,
- **Dezirae**, Deziree, Origin: French, Meaning: Desired, Likeness of God
- **Daly**, Dalten, Origin: Irish, Meaning: Assembly, Bringer of Light
- **Denzel**, Danzel, Danzell,
- **Dolly**, Dollee, Dolli,
- **Dempsey**, Dempsie, Origin: Irish, Meaning: Proud, Honorable
- **Dorian**, Doriana,
- **Danika**, Dannika, Origin: Slavic, Meaning: Morning Star Attentive
- **Demica**, Demicah, Origin: French, Meaning: Friendly, Seeker of Truth

- **Darielle**, Dariel, Darriel,
- **Dion**, see Deon
- **Delaynie**, Dellaney, Origin: Irish, Meaning: Of the Champion, Victorious
- **Daron**, Darron, Daryn,
- **Drake**, Drago, Origin: Latin, Meaning: Dragon, Symbol
- **Delmar**, Dalmar, Origin: Latin, Meaning: By the Sea, Filled With Praise
- **Daniela**, Daniele, Daniell,
- **Dallan**, Daelan, Daelen,
- **Daelin**, Dalian, Daylan,
- **Derek,** Darek, Darik,
- **Dorran,** Dorren, Origin: Hebrew, Meaning: God's Gift, Sacrifice
- **Dennis**, Dennes, Denny, Origin: Greek, Meaning: Happy, Effective
- **Dee**, Dede, Deedee, Origin: Welsh, Meaning: Dark Loving
- **Daymian**, Origin: Russian, Meaning: Soother, One Who Restores
- **Deaundre**, Deondre, Origin: French, Meaning: Courageous, Submissive
- **Daphne,** Daphaney,

- **Danelle,** Danel, Danele,
- **Denae**, Denay, Denee
- **Demetria,**
- **Davina,** Davina, Dava,
- **Delta**, Origin: Greek, Meaning: Door, Seeker of Truth
- **Dasan**, Dassan, Origin: Pomo, Meaning: Leader, Chosen
- **Dana**, Daina, Danah,
- **Devine**, Devyn, Origin: Irish, Meaning: Poet, Seeker of Wisdom
- **Deidra**, Deidre, Dierdra,
- **Davonn**, Davontay,
- **Dollie,** Origin: American, Meaning: Compassionate, Christlike
- **Doran,** Dorin, Doron,
- **Dacey**, Dacee, Daci,
- **Di,** Diahann, Dianah,
- **Dayvid**, Origin: Hebrew, Meaning: Beloved, Lover of All
- **Daria**, Darria, Darya, Origin: Greek, Meaning: Wealthy, Gracious
- **Daylen**, Daylin, Origin: English, Meaning: From the Dale, Secure

- **Dolan**, Dolin, Dolyn, Origin: Irish, Meaning: Dark-Haired, Full of Life
- **Dori**, Dorie, Dorrie,
- **Darrell**, Darelle, Daril,
- **Damaris**, Damarius,
- **Dawnya**, Danya,
- **Demetric**, Demetrik,
- **Darrien**, Darrin, Deren,
- **Dolph,** Dolf, Origin: Slavic, Meaning: Famous, Great
- **Darren**, Daran, Daren,
- **Deontee**, Deontre, Dion,
- **Dmetrius**
- **Darnall**, Darnell, Origin: Irish, Meaning: Magnificent, Loving
- **Dawne**, Dawnn, Dawnna,
- **Deandre**, D'Andre,
- **Devona**, Devonda,
- **Delicia**, Deleesha,
- **Dasha**, Dashah, Dasya, Origin: Russian, Meaning: Divine, Display Miracle,
- **Douglass**, Origin: Scottish, Meaning: From the Dark Stream, Adventurous
- **Demitrik**, Demitrias

- **Daisy**, Daisee, Origin: Old German, Meaning: Vision of the Day, Cleansed
- **Dacie**, Dacy, Daicee,
- **Darius**, Darian, Dariann,
- **Dacian**, Dalbert, Del,
- **Delisha,** Delysia, Origin: Latin, Meaning: Delightful, Joyous Spirit
- **Debbi**, Debbie, Debbora,
- **Denise**, Danice, Deni,
- **Darsie**, Origin: French, Meaning: Fortress, Established in Strength
- **Deeanna,** Origin: Latin, Meaning: Divine, Brightness of the Dawn
- **Darbie,** Origin: Irish, Meaning: Freedom, Free Spirit
- **Damon**, Daemon,
- **Delany**, Dalaney,
- **Damian**, Daemien,
- **Delana**, Dalanna,
- **Dixie**, Dixee, Dixi, Dixy, Origin: French, Meaning: Tenth, Blessing
- **Delbert**, Origin: English, Meaning: Bright as Day, Obedient
- **Damiana**, Damianna, Origin: Greek, Meaning: Soother, Healer

- **Dylan**, Dyllan, Dyllon,
- **Dameon**, Damian,
- **Darcy**, Darcee, Darcey,
- **Dora,** Doralia, Doralie, Origin: Greek, Meaning: Gift of God, Wise
- **Debborah**, Debby, Debi,
- **Darling**, Origin: French, Meaning: Darling, Loving
- **Davonte,** Dayvin
- **Donna**, Origin: Old English, Meaning: Beginning Anew, Joy and Praise
- **Donovan**, Donavan,
- **Demetra,** Demitra, Origin: Greek, Meaning: Plentiful, Fruitful
- **Davison**, Origin: English, Meaning: Honorable, Loving
- **Diamond**, Diamonique,
- **Dinah**, Dina, Dyna,
- **Doreen**, Dorene, Dorey,
- **Dominique**, Dominica,
- **Daron**, Darius, Deron, Origin: Irish, Meaning: Great, Esteemed
- **Dunstan**, Dunsten, Origin: English, Meaning: From the Stony Hill, Victorious

- **Danielle**, Origin: French, Meaning: God Is My Judge, Discerning
- **Dellia**, Delya, Origin: Greek, Meaning: Visible, Divine Reflection
- **Darrah**, Origin: Hebrew, Meaning: Compassionate, Bearer of Mercy
- **Dandre,** De Andre,
- **Douglas**, Doug,
- **Dania**, Danee, Dani,

E

- **Edana**, Edanna, Edena, Origin: Irish, Meaning: Ardent Flame, Unending Love
- **Erin,** Erine, Erinn,
- **Elynn**, Elinn, Elyne,
- **Ella**, Ellah, Origin: Old German, Meaning: Beautiful, Sustained
- **Eryka**, Erykka, Origin: Old Norse, Meaning: Brave, Victorious
- **Ellison**, Elison, Ellyson, Origin: English, Meaning: Son of the Redeemed, One Near to God's Heart
- **Ellise**, Ellyce, Ellyse,
- **Eira**, Eirah, Welsh, Meaning: Snow, Pure
- **Elisha**, Elishah, Elishia,
- **Elliot,** Eliot, Eliott, Elliott, Origin: Hebrew, Meaning: The Lord Is My God, Consecrated
- **Esme**, Esmee, Origin: French, Meaning: Overcomer, Victor
- **Electra**, Elektra, Origin: Greek, Meaning: Brilliant, Eternal Hope
- **Emilie**, Emillie, Emilly,

- **Ephron,** Origin: Hebrew, Meaning: Strong, Thankful
- **Evita,** Eveeta, Origin: Hispanic, Meaning: Youthful Life, Childlike
- **Emil,** Emill, Origin: German, Meaning: Industrious, Diligent Seeker
- **Emilian**, Emille, Emils, Origin: Polish, Meaning: Eager, Purified
- **Ellissa**, Ellisia, Ellyssa,
- **Eleanor**, Eleanore,
- **Edin**, Edyn, Origin: Hebrew, Meaning: Delightful, Pleasing
- **Elton**, Alten, Alton, Ellton, Origin: English, Meaning: From the Old Town, Steadfast
- **Edna,** Ednah, Origin: Hebrew, Meaning: Rejuvenated, Filled With Pleasure
- **Evangeline**, Evangelina, Origin: Greek, Meaning: Bringer of Good News, Happy Messenger
- **Eriq,** Erric, Errick, Errick,
- **Evelyn**, Evalina, Evaline,
- **Etienne,** Etiene, Origin: French, Meaning: Enthroned, Humble
- **Elise**, Elisse, Ellice,

- **Erhard,** Erhardt, Erhart, Origin: German, Meaning: Resolute, Efficient
- **Estrella**, Estelina,
- **Eda**, Edah, Origin: Irish, Meaning: Loyal, Faithful
- **Enrique**, Origin: Spanish, Meaning: Head of the Household, Servant
- **Eve**, Eva, Evah, Evie, Origin: Hebrew, Meaning: Mother of Life, Full of Life
- **Elizabeth**, Elisabeth,
- **Emilyann**, Emilyanne, Origin: American, Meaning: Gracious, Thoughtful
- **Elden**, Eldin, Origin: Old English, Meaning: Wise, Guardian, Good Judgment
- **Ellen**, Elen, Ellan, Ellin, Origin: English, Meaning: Bright Heir
- **Emmi**, Emmie, Origin: English, Meaning: Striving, Attentive
- **Emilio**, Emillio, Origin: Italian, Meaning: Glorifier, Obedient
- **Ernst**, Origin: English, Meaning: Sincere, Free in Spirit
- **Emerson**, Emmerson, Origin: English, Meaning: Son of the Leader, Victorious

- **Ethel**, Ethyl, Origin: Old English, Meaning: One of High Regard, Noble
- **Evin**, Evyn, Origin: Irish, Meaning: Young Warrior, Noble Protector
- **Erica**, Arica, Aricka,
- **Evelynne**, Origin: English, Meaning: Hazelnut, Radiant
- **Elisabethe**, Origin: Hebrew, Meaning: Oath of God, Consecrated
- **Ernest**, Ernesto, Ernie,
- **Eagan**, see Egan
- **Einar**, Ejnar, Origin: Old Norse, Meaning: Individualist, Free
- **Egan,** Eagan, Egann,
- **Elgin,** Elgen, Origin: English, Meaning: Noble, Responsible
- **Erikka**, Errica, Errika,
- **Enrique**, Enrico, Enrikos,
- **Estee**, Origin: English, Meaning: Star, Fulfillment
- **Elva**, Elvia
- **Elaine**, Elain, Elane,
- **Eleena**, Elina, Ellena, Origin: Russian, Meaning: Radiant, Illuminated
- **Elias**, Ellis, Origin: Greek, Meaning: God Is My Salvation, Mouthpiece of God

- **Elainna,** Elani, Elania,
- **Ellis**, see Elias
- **Everette**, Everitt, Origin: German, Meaning: Courageous, Unending Praise
- **Ezra**, Esera, Esra, Ezera,
- **Eddy**, Eduardo, Edwardo,
- **Emmet**, Emitt, Emmett,
- **Elissa**, Lissa, Origin: Latin, Meaning: Sweetly Blissful, Strong Faith
- **Emanuel**, Emanual,
- **Eric,** Aric, Arik, Arick,
- **Elinor**, Ellenora, Elynora, Origin: Greek, Meaning: Bright as the Sun, Kindhearted
- **Emelia**, Amilia, Emalia,
- **Earl,** Earle, Origin: English, Meaning: Noble, Reflected Image
- **Eirenna**, Origin: English, Meaning: Peace, Contentment
- **Ebonee**, Eboney, Ebonie, Origin: American, Meaning: Hard, Dark Wood Shining
- **Ellie**, Elie, Elli, Origin: Estonian, Meaning: Illuminated, Shining Light
- **Enrica**, Enrikka, Origin: French, Meaning: Home Ruler, Righteous

- **Eladah**, Eilada, Elada,
- **Ennis**, Enis
- **Easton**, Eason, Origin: English, Meaning: From the Eastern Town, Christlike
- **Eden**, Eaden, Eadin,
- **Edith**, Edythe, Origin: Old English, Meaning: Valuable, Gift Wise
- **Eli**, Ely, Origin: Hebrew, Meaning: Uplifted, Delivered
- **Eyota**, Eyotah, Origin: Native American, Meaning: Greatest, Servant
- **Emma**, Ema, Origin: Old German, Meaning: All-Embracing, Absolute Faith
- **Esmunde**, Origin: Old English, Meaning: Rich Protector, Gracious
- **Elissa**, Elisia, Ellisa,
- **Emiliann**, Emilianne,
- **Eldon**, Elldon, Origin: English, Meaning: From the Holy Hill, Enlightened
- **Emile**, Emilee, Emiley,
- **Emmy**, Emee, Emi,
- **Elysa,** Elyssa
- **Emanuell,** Emmanuel,
- **Emery**, Emeri, Emmery,
- **Emily**, Emalee, Emelie,

- **Estelle**, Estele, Origin: French, Meaning: Star, Infinite Potential
- **Edwin**, Edwyn, Edwina, Origin: Old English, Meaning: Prosperous Friend, Belonging to God
- **Eldridge**, Eldredge, Origin: German, Meaning: Mature Counselor, Godly
- **Eliah,** Eliyah, Origin: Hebrew, Meaning: The Lord Is God, Believer
- **Elvira**, Elvera, Origin: Spanish, Meaning: Fair, Wise
- **Elana**, Elaina, Elaina,
- **Edgar**, Ed, Origin: English, Meaning: Prosperous, Gifted
- **Esau,** Esaw, Origin: Hebrew, Meaning: Hairy Strength
- **Emery**, Origin: Turkish, Meaning: Brother God's, Servant
- **Emerald**, Emeralde, Origin: French, Meaning: Green Gem, Breathtaking
- **Eunice**, Eunique, Eunise, Origin: Greek, Meaning: Joyous, Victorious
- **Ember,** Embur (see also
- **Emmott**, Origin: Old English, Meaning: Earnest, Genuine, Devotion

- **Emily**, Origin: Latin, Meaning: Industrious, Blessed
- **Ellynn**, Origin: American, Meaning: Clear Pool, Cleansed
- **Eythan**, Origin: Hebrew, Meaning: Firmness, Steadfast in Truth
- **Emmelie**, Emylee
- **Erwin**, see Irwin
- **Estelita**, Estella, Estrela,
- **Erinne,** Erin, Eryn, Erynn,
- **Edward**, Ed, Eddie,
- **Edmund**, Edmon,
- **Elan**, Elann
- **Elasya**, Origin: Hebrew, Meaning: God Has Created, Image of God
- **Edmond**, Edmonde,
- **Elijah**, Elija, Eliyahu, Origin: Hebrew, Meaning: The Lord Is My God, Spiritual Champion
- **Easter**, Eastre, Origin: Old German, Meaning: Spring Festival, Celebration
- **Everlee**, Everleigh, Origin: English, Meaning: From the Boar Meadow, Faithful
- **Ethan**, Eathan, Ethen,
- **Esmond**, Origin: Old English, Meaning: Blessed, Peace, Prosperous Protector

- **Eugene**, Gene, Origin: Greek, Meaning: Born to Nobility, Vivacious
- **Eliora**, Eliaura, Eliorra,
- **Emilianna**, Emiliana,
- **Enos**, Enosh, Origin: Hebrew, Meaning: Man, Expectant
- **Elvis**, Elvys, Origin: Old Norse, Meaning: All-Wise, Righteous

F

- > **Fabia**, Fabiana,
- > **Fabian,** Fabayan,
- > **Fabianna**, Fabianne,
- > **Fabiano**, Fabien, Fabio,
- > **Fabria**, Fabriana,
- > **Falina**, Falena, Faylina,
- > **Falyn,** Origin: Irish, Meaning: Grandchild of the Ruler, Heir
- > **Fannie**, Origin: English, French, Meaning: Dedicated
- > **Fanny,** Fanney, Fanni,
- > **Fanya,** Fania, Fannia, Origin: Russian, Meaning: Free, Vindicated
- > **Farron**, Farryn, Faryn
- > **Felecia**, Felicya,
- > **Felicity,** Felicianna,
- > **Felina**, Origin: Latin, Meaning: Catlike, Upright
- > **Felipe**, see Phillip
- > **Felisha,** Origin: Latin, Meaning: Fortunate, Joyful

- **Felissa,** Feliza, Felysse, Origin: English, Meaning: Joyful, Content
- **Felix**, see Phillip, Origin: Latin, Meaning: Fortunate, Blessed
- **Felton**, Felten, Origin: English, Meaning: From the Field Town, Hopeful
- **Fenton,** Fenny, Origin: English, Meaning: From the Marshland, Spirit of Life
- **Ferdinand**, Ferdnand, Origin: Gothic, Meaning: Adventurous, Seeker of Truth
- **Ferell,** Ferryl, Origin: Irish, Meaning: Valiant, Servant
- **Feris**, Origin: Middle Eastern, Meaning: Horseman, Fearsome
- **Finian**, Phinean, Origin: Irish, Meaning: Fair Hero, Servant
- **Fiona,** Fionna, Origin: Irish, Meaning: Fair, Persevering
- **Fletcher**, Flecher, Fletch Origin: Anglo-Saxon, Meaning: Arrow Featherer, Ingenious
- **Flora,** Floria, Floriana,
- **Florann**, Floren, Florida,
- **Florence**, Flo, Florance,

- ➤ **Florian**, Florien, Florrian, Origin: English, Meaning: Blooming, Nourished
- ➤ **Florianna**, Origin: Latin, Meaning: Flower, Nurtured
- ➤ **Florrie**, Flossie, Origin: Latin, Meaning: Flourishing, Prosperous
- ➤ **Floyd**, Floydd, Origin: Welsh, Meaning: White-or-Gray-Haired, Wise
- ➤ **Flynn**, Flinn, Flyn, Origin: Gaelic, Meaning: Son of Redhead, Blessed
- ➤ **Fontana**, Origin: French, Meaning: Fountain, Sustained
- ➤ **Fontanna,** Fontaine,
- ➤ **Forbes**, Forbe, Origin: Gaelic, Meaning: Prosperous Blessed
- ➤ **Forrest,** Forest, Forster,
- ➤ **Frazer**, Frazier, Origin: French, Meaning: Strawberry, Filled With Life
- ➤ **Frederica**, Freddi,
- ➤ **Frederick**, Origin: German, Meaning: Peaceful Ruler, Perceptive
- ➤ **Fredericka**, Frederina,
- ➤ **Frederique**, Fredrika, Origin: Old German, Meaning: Peaceful Ruler, Compassionate

- **Freia,** Frieda, Origin: German, Meaning: Serene, Victorious
- **Freida**, Freda, Freeda,
- **Freja**, Fraya, Freya, Origin: Swedish, Virtuous, Woman Valuable

G

- **Gavyn**, Origin: Welsh, Meaning: White Hawk, Content
- **Galvin**, Galvan, Galven, Origin: Gaelic, Meaning: Glowing, Blessed
- **Gracia**, Graciana, Gracie, Origin: Latin, Meaning: Patient, Full of Grace
- **Ginah,** Ginia (see also
- **Galiena**, Galienna, Origin: Old German, Meaning: Supreme, Respectful
- **Grayson**, Greyson, Origin: Middle Eastern, Meaning: Son of the Bailiff, One of Knowledge
- **Gregory,** Greg, Gregg,
- **Georgeanna,** Georgene,
- **Genna**, see Jenna
- **Gerald,** Geraldo,
- **Greggory**, Gregori, Greig,
- **Gloria**, Gloriela,

- **Gilbert**, Gibb, Gibbs, Gil,
- **Gary**, Garry, Origin: German, Meaning: Mighty, Regenerated
- **Grace**, Gracey, Graci,
- **Gustaf**, Gustav,
- **Gino**, Geno, Origin: Greek, Meaning: Of Noteworthy Birth, Delivered
- **Gustavus**, Origin: Scandinavian, Meaning: God's Staff, Blessed
- **Gilda**, Gilde, Origin: Anglo-Saxon, Meaning: Covered With Gold, Blessed
- **Gillian**, see Jillian
- **Gavin,** Gavan, Gaven,
- **Garvin**, Garvan, Garvyn, Origin: English, Meaning: Friend in Battle, Peaceful
- **Gabriel**, Gab, Gabe,
- **Geneva**, Jeneva, Origin: French, Meaning: Juniper Tree, Wise
- **Gladys**, Gladis, Origin: Irish, Meaning: Princess, Spiritual Understanding
- **Gilmore**, Gilmour, Origin: Irish, Meaning: Devout, Dependent
- **Gabriela,** Gabriele,

- **Ganya**, Gania, Ganyah, Origin: Hebrew, Meaning: Garden of God, Refreshed
- **Gena,** see Gina
- **Gannen**, Origin: Irish, Meaning: White, Devout
- Gaston, Gascon, Gaston, Origin: French, Meaning: From Gascony, Protected
- **Gordon,** Gordan,
- **Grant**, Grantham,
- **Glenna,** Glenda, Origin: Irish, Meaning: From The Valley, Blooming
- **Gibson,** Gilson, Origin: English, Meaning: Son of the Honest Man, Fruitful
- **Gabriello**, Gibbbee,
- **Gustave**, Gus, Guss,
- **Grady**, Gradey, Origin: Gaelic, Meaning: Noble, Strong
- **Gianna**, Gianna,
- **Gabriell**, Gabrielli,
- **Galina**, Gailina, Origin: Russian, Meaning: Shining, Glorified
- **Gabrielle**, Gabbey,
- **Gannon,** Gannan,
- **Gerrett** (Jarrett), Origin: Irish, Meaning: Warrior, Free

- **Gabriala**, Gabralla,
- **Gina**, Geena, Gena,
- **Gabriella**, Origin: Hebrew, Meaning: Devoted to God, Confident
- **Gemina**, Gemmina Origin: Greek, Meaning: Twin Righteous
- **Gabriana**, Gabrianna,
- **Gloriella**, Glorielle, Glory,
- **Geneen**, see Jeanine
- **George**, Georges,
- **Geffrey**, Geoff, Geoffrey,
- **Gene**, see Eugene
- **Gareth**, Garith, Garreth, Origin: Welsh, Meaning: Gentle Peaceful
- **Glendon**, Glenden, **Origin:** Scottish, Meaning: From the Valley Fortress, Excellent Worth
- **Gizelle**, Gissele, Giselle,
- **Genevieve**, Genavieve,
- **Gennifer,** see Jennifer
- **Gibbie,** Origin: Hebrew, Meaning: Devoted to God, Brave
- **Gemini**, Gemelle,

- **Geary**, Gearey, Origin: English, Meaning: Changeable, Courageous
- **Gayle**, Origin: Old English, Meaning: My Father, Rejoices, Lively
- **Gerry,** Jeraldine, Origin: Old German, Meaning: Powerful, Victorious
- **Geraldine**, Geraldina,
- **Garner**, Garnier, Origin: French, Meaning: Guard One of Integrity
- **Gresham**, Grisham, Origin: English, Meaning: From the Village by the Pasture Peaceful
- **Godfrey**, Godfry
- **Geoffrey,** Geffery,
- **Ginny**, Gini, Ginni,

H

- **Hannen**, Hannon, Origin: Hebrew, Meaning: Merciful, Compassionate
- **Howell,** Howel, Origin: Welsh, Meaning: Remarkable Reconciled
- **Harper**, Harpo, Origin: English, Meaning: Harp Player, Instrument of Praise
- **Herick,** Herrik, Origin: German, Meaning: War Ruler, Chosen
- **Hilda**, Hilde, Origin: Old German, Meaning: Battle Maid, Courageous
- **Hamlet**, Hamlett, Origin: Old Norse, Meaning: From the Village, Compassionate
- **Hartley,** Hartlee,
- **Haley,** Halley, Halli, Hally, Origin: Nigerian, Meaning: Unexpected Gift, Blessing
- **Hensley**, Origin: English, Meaning: From the High Pasture Protector, Shepard
- **Hamilton**, Hamelton, Origin: Old English, Meaning: From the Fortified Castle, Faithful

- **Heidi**, Heide, Heidee,
- **Hollis**, Hollyss, Origin: Old English, Meaning: From the Holly Trees, Righteous
- **Hugh**, Huey, Hughes,
- **Holden**, Holdin, Origin: English, Meaning: From the Valley Hollow Fearless
- **Haywood**, Heywood, Origin: English, Meaning: From the Hedged, Forest Chosen
- **Haydon** (see also
- **Hal**, see Harold
- **Halen**, Haylan, Origin: Swedish, Meaning: Hall, Gracious
- **Hope**, Hopie, Origin: Old English, Meaning: Trust in the Future, Understanding Heart
- **Harris**, Harrison, Origin: Old English, Meaning: Son of the Strong Man, Courageous
- **Holbrook**, Holbrooke, Origin: Old English, Meaning: From the Brook, Peaceful
- **Heather,** Heatherlee, Origin: Middle English, Meaning: Flowering, Blooming Cover of Beauty
- **Hillary**, Hilaree, Hilari,
- **Hilton,** Hillton, Origin: English, Meaning: From the Hill Town, Obedient
- **Henry**, Hank, Henri,

- **Holli**, Hollie, Origin: Old English, Meaning: Holly Tree, Peaceful
- **Hugo,** Origin: Old German, Meaning: Thoughtful, Wise
- **Helen**, Hellen, Origin: Greek, Meaning: Light, Righteous
- **Hilary**, Hillaree, Hillarie,
- **Howard,** Howie, Origin: English, Meaning: Chief Guardian Discerning
- **Harriet**, Harriett, Hattie, Origin: Old German, Meaning: Ruler of the Household, Discerner of Excellence
- **Holly**, Hollee, Holley,
- **Haven**, Havan, Havin, Origin: Dutch, Meaning: Harbor, Preserved
- **Hana**, Hanita, Origin: Japanese, Meaning: Flower, Joyful
- **Harley**, Harlee, Harleigh, Origin: Old English, Meaning: From the Rabbit Pasture, Chosen of God
- **Harry**, Harray, Harrey, Origin: Old German, Meaning: Home Ruler, Integrity
- **Heinrich**, Heinrick,

- **Hayes**, Hays, Origin: English, Meaning: From the Hedged Valley, Moderate
- **Harmonie**, Origin: Latin, Meaning: Oneness, Unifier
- **Harmony**, Harmoni,
- **Hilleree**, Hillory, Origin: English, Meaning: Cheerful, Blessed
- **Heath**, Heathe, Origin: English, Meaning: Shrub, Protector
- **Hercules**, Origin: Greek, Meaning: Glorious, Gift Enduring
- **Harvey**, Harv
- **Hardin**, Hardan, Origin: English, Meaning: From the Hares' Valley, Righteous
- **Hanan**, Hannan,
- **Harvey**, Origin: French, Meaning: Warrior, Steadfast
- **Hayden**, Haden, Haydn,
- **Helena**, Haleena,
- **Harold**, Hal, Herald,
- **Hannah**, Hanna, Origin: Hebrew, Meaning: Gracious, Compassionate
- **Henley**, see Hanley
- **Herman**, Hermann,

- **Henrietta**, Henrieta, Origin: English, Meaning: Household Ruler, Strong
- **Hogan**, Hogen, Origin: Gaelic, Meaning: Youthful, Generous
- **Hollyann**, Hollianna,
- **Hector**, Hectar, Origin: Greek, Meaning: Steadfast, One of Integrity
- **Haniel**, Hanniel, Origin: Hebrew, Meaning: Grace of God, Restored
- **Halena**, Helana,
- **Hardy**, Origin: English, Meaning: Bold, Confident

I

- **Idalia,** Idalis, Idalys, Origin: American, Meaning: Creative, Gifted
- **Isadora**, Isidora, Isidora, Origin: Greek, Meaning: Gift of the Goddess, Inspired
- **Irwin**, Erwin, Erwyn,
- **Ivy,** Ivey, Ivie, Origin: English, Meaning: Ivy Plant, Trusting
- **Ingemar**, Ingeborg, Origin: Old Norse, Meaning: Famous Son, Adventurous
- **Izaak**, Izac, Izak, Izakk,
- **Ian**, Ean, Iain, Origin: Scottish, Meaning: God Is Gracious, Discreet
- **Ingram**, Ingraham,
- **Inger**, Ing, Inga, Inge, Origin: Old Norse, Meaning: Army of the Son, Kind
- **Ida**, Idaleena, Idarina, Origin: German, Meaning: Youth, Industrious
- **Ingerlisa**, Ingerlise, Origin: Norwegian, Meaning: Praised Daughter, Consecrated to God

- **Imla**, Imlah, Origin: Hebrew, Meaning: Fulfilling, Prosperous
- **India**, Indya, Origin: English, Meaning: From India, Gift of Faith
- **Irwyn**, Origin: Old English, Meaning: Friend, Triumphant Spirit
- **Ioanna**, Ioana, Origin: Russian, Meaning: God Is Gracious, Set Apart
- **Iola**, Iolia, Origin: Greek, Meaning: Dawn of Day, One Made Worthy
- **Izabelle**, Origin: Spanish, Meaning: Consecrated to God, Discerning Spirit
- **Ilya**, Ilias, Iljah
- **Iman,** Imani, Origin: Middle Eastern, Meaning: Believer, Illuminated
- **Ina,** Inah, Origin: Irish, Meaning: Pure, Divine Inspiration
- **Ivana**, Ivania, Ivanna, Origin: Slavic, Meaning: God Is Gracious, Thankful
- **Ivar,** Iver, Ivor, Origin: Old Norse, Meaning: Noble, Peaceful
- **Ianos**, Iano, Ianos, Origin: Czech, Meaning: God Is Gracious, Divine Vision

- ➤ **Ioan,** Ioann, Origin: Romanian, Meaning: God Is Gracious, Cherished
- ➤ **Imelda**, Imalda, Origin: Swiss, Meaning: All-Encompassing, Battle Victorious
- ➤ **Iris**, Irisa, Irisha, Irissa,
- ➤ **Irina,** Irana, Iriana,
- ➤ **Isabelle**, Izabel, Izabele,
- ➤ **Isaac,** Ike, Isaak, Isac,
- ➤ **Iona**, Ione, Ionia, Origin: Greek, Meaning: Violet Flower, Inner Beauty
- ➤ **Immanuel**, Immanuela,
- ➤ **Ira,** Irah, Origin: Hebrew, Meaning: Watchful Led by the Spirit
- ➤ **Ilana,** Ilani, Illana,
- ➤ **Isaiah**, Ishmael, Ishmeil,
- ➤ **Ivan,** Iven, Origin: Russian, Meaning: God Is Gracious, Triumphant
- ➤ **Izzy**, Yitzak, Yitzhak, Origin: Hebrew, Meaning: Laughter, Child of Promise
- ➤ **Irving**, Earvin, Erv,
- ➤ **Ingrim,** Origin: Old Norse, Meaning: King's Raven, Wise
- ➤ **Iolana**, Ioanna, Origin: Hawaiian, Meaning: Soaring Like a Hawk, Steadfast

- **Ilan**, Illan, Origin: Hebrew, Meaning: Youth, Pride of the Father
- **Iwan**, Iwann, Origin: Polish, Meaning: God Is Gracious Grateful
- **Isak**, Ishaq, Itzak, Izaac,
- **Ilona**, Ileena, Ilina, Origin: Hungarian, Meaning: Light, Disciple of Christ
- **Iliana**, Ileana, Illiana
- **Ivonne**, Ivette, Ivete,
- **Ivory**, Ivori, Origin: American, Meaning: Made of Ivory, Fearless
- **Illanda**, Illani, Origin: Hebrew, Meaning: Tree, Firmly Rooted
- **Ingrid**, Ingela, Origin: Old Norse, Meaning: Hero's Daughter, Cherished
- **Isabel,** Isabela, Isabella,

J

- **Juliana**, Juliane, Juliann,
- **Jonah**, Jona, Jonas,
- **Julian**, Juliano, Julias,
- **Jarvis**, Jarvas, Jarvares,
- **Jiovanni,** Jovaan, Jovani,
- **Janessa,** Janiesha,
- **Jasmin**, Jasmon,
- **Jeroham**, Jeroam, Origin: Hebrew, Meaning: Loved, Treasured
- **Jimelle,** Origin: Hebrew, Meaning: Handsome, Image of God
- **John,** Origin: Hebrew, Meaning: Gift of the Lord, God's Precious Gift
- **Janzen,** Jensen, Origin: Scandinavian, Meaning: Son of Jan, Joyful
- **Jolinn,** Jolynn, Origin: English, Meaning: God Will Increase Reborn,
- **Joseseph**, Jose', Jose'e,
- **Jeanine**, Jeannette,

- **Jeffrey**, Jefery, Jeff,
- **Janan**, Janani, Janann, Origin: Middle Eastern, Meaning: Tenderhearted, Gentle
- **Jinny**, see Ginny
- **Julius**, Jule, Jules,
- **Joseph**, Joe, Joey,
- **Jake**, Jayke, Origin: English, Meaning: Substitute, New Covenant
- **Jesse**, Jesee, Jess,
- **Jocelyn**, Jocelin,
- **Jameson**, Jamerson,
- **Jaison**, Jasan, Jasen,
- **Jacqueline**, Jacalyn,
- **Jarell,** Jarel, Jarelle,
- **Jenney**, Jennie,
- **Jael**, Jaela, Jaelle (see
- **Jaelynn**, Jalen, Jalin,
- **Jason**, Jacen, Jaeson,
- **Jasmaine**, Jasman,
- **Justine**, Justinna, Origin: French, Meaning: Upright, Righteous
- **Jacobi**, Jackobi, Origin: Scottish, Meaning: Replacement, Joyous

- **Jan**, Jani, Jania, Jann, Origin: German, Meaning: God's Gift, Cherished
- **Janea**, Janay, Jannay,
- **Jane**, Jaine, Janet,
- **Julietta**, Juliette, Julliet,
- **Joelle**, Joella, Origin: French, Meaning: The Lord Is My God, Beloved
- **Johann**, Joannes,
- **Jenniffer**, Jenny, Origin: Welsh, Meaning: Fair, Trusting
- **Julia**, Julee, Juleen, Juli,
- **Jamian,** Jamiel, Jaymin, Origin: Hebrew, Meaning: Favored, Triumphant
- **Jamila**, Jahmela,
- **Jina**, Jinna (see also
- **Jullietta**, Origin: French, Meaning: Youthful, Immovable
- **Jonathan**, Johnathan,
- **Johannas**, Johanes,
- **Jacquelyn**, Jacquelynn,
- **Jamelya**, Jamilia,
- **Jacon** (see also Jaakan), Origin: Hebrew, Meaning: Trouble, Victorious
- **Jasper**, Jaspar, Origin: English, Meaning: Treasure Holder, Richly Blessed

- **Jassmine**, Jassmyn, Jaz,
- **Janell**, Janella, Janiel,
- **James**, Jaimes, Jaymes,
- **Jilanna**, see Gianna
- **Jordan**, Jordaan,
- **Jamii**, Jammie, Jamya,
- **Janette**, Jannine,
- **Jacques**, Jacquan,
- **Jaycie**, Jaciel, Jayce,
- **Julien**, Julio, Jullian, Origin: Latin, Meaning: Youthful, Regenerated
- **Jeanette**, Janeen,
- **Jack**, Jackie, Jacky, Jax, Origin: English, Meaning: God Is Gracious, Redeemed
- **Jessica**, Jesi, Jesica,
- **Julianna,** Julie, Julieann,
- **Jeaneen,** Jeanett,
- **Jolan**, Jolanda, Jolanta, Origin: Hungarian, Meaning: Violet Flower, Steady Growth
- **Jady**, Jaide, Jayde, Origin: Spanish, Meaning: Precious Gem, Priceless
- **Jackson**, Jakson, Jaxon, Origin: English, Meaning: Son of Jack, Gracious
- **Janae**, Janaya, Janaya,

- **Jaime,** Jaimey, Jaimee,
- **Jillene,** Jilliana, Jillianne,
- **Justinn,** Justinus, Juston,
- **Jeannine,** Jenine, Origin: French, Meaning: God Is Gracious, Preserved
- **Jeremii,** Origin: English, Meaning: God Is Exalted, Humble
- **Jessie**, Jessika, Jessy,
- **Johana,** see Joanna
- **Jamie,** Jamee, Jamey,
- **Jaya**, Jaea, Jaia, Jayla,
- **Juliene**, Julienne, Julila,
- **Jeremee**, Jeremey,
- **Josephine**, Jo, Joey,
- **Jackee**, Jacki, Jacklyn,
- **Jacob,** Jacobb, Jacobs,
- **Janice**, Janis, Jannie,
- **Jeremy**, Jeramee,
- **Juliet,** Julieta, Juliete,
- **Jade,** Jadah, Jadi, Jadie,
- **Justin,** Justan, Justen,
- **Jelani**, Jeanee, Jelani,
- **Jadon**, Jaden, Jadin,
- **Justun**, Justyn, Origin: Latin, Meaning: Upright, Righteous

- **Jilian**, Jiliana, Jiliann,
- **Josephina**, Josey, Josie, Origin: French
- **Joselyn,** Origin: Old German, Meaning: Joyous, Righteous
- **Juri** (see Yuri)
- **Josephus,** Jozef, Yosef,
- **Jamilla**, Yamila, Origin: Middle Eastern, Meaning: Beautiful, Loving
- **Jullianna**, Origin: Latin, Meaning: Youthful, Guided by Faith
- **Julisa**, Julissa, Julliana,
- **Jodey**, Jodi, Jodie,
- **Janelle,** Janel, Janele,
- **Justinna**, Origin: Hebrew, Meaning: Just, Righteous
- **Jeremiah**, Jeramiah,
- **Jilianna,** Jill, Jillana,
- **Jacey**, J.C., Jace, Jacee,
- **Jeremia,** Jeremias,
- **Janielle,** Jannel, Jannell,
- **Jolene,** Jolayne, Jolean,
- **Justina**, Justeen,
- **Jana,** Janna (see also
- **Jillian**, Gillian, Jil,

- **Jennifer**, Jen, Jenefer,
- **Jin**, Jinn, Origin: Chinese, Meaning: Gold, True Worth
- **Jasmine**, Jas, Jasmain,
- **Jay**, Jey, Origin: Old French, Meaning: Vivacious, Adventurous
- **Julilla**, Julina, Juline,
- **Jeffery**, Jeffrie, Jeffries,
- **Jami,** Jamia, Jamian,
- **Janett,** Janey, Janie,
- **Jimmie**, Jimmy, Jimy, Origin: Hebrew, Meaning: Supplanter, Nurtured
- **Jamelia**, Jamelle,
- **Joel,** Jole, Origin: Hebrew, Meaning: The Lord Is My God, God's Messenger
- **Joshua**, Jeshua,
- **Jaycee,** Jaycey, Jaycie
- **Jada**, Jaeda, Jaida,
- **Jacy**, Jaicy
- **Joan,** Joane, Joana, JoAnna,
- **Joleane**, Joleen, Joline,
- **Jamiel,** Jamil, Jamill,
- **Joannah**, Joey,
- **Jazmin,** Jazmine,

- **Jewel,** Jewell, Jewelle, Origin: French, Meaning: Gem, Precious
- **Joah**, Yoah, Origin: Hebrew, Meaning: God Is Gracious, Secure
- **Joachim**, Joakim,
- **Jim**, Jimi, Jimmee,
- **Jindrich**, Jindrick, Origin: Czech, Meaning: Head of the Household, Trusted
- **June,** Junelle, Junia, Origin: Latin, Meaning: Born in the Forth Month, Loving
- **Jillisa**, Origin: Latin, Meaning: Youthful, Regenerated

K

- **Katy**, Catey, Caytee,
- **Katrin**, Katrine, Katrinia,
- **Kira**, Kiri, Kiria, Kirianna,
- **Kierlyn,** Kierlynn, Kierra,
- **Kara**, Kaira, Kairah,
- **Kimberly**, Kim, Kimba,
- **Kayleen**, Caeleen,
- **Katica**, Katja, Katka,
- **Kailee,** Kailey, see
- **Karrianne,** Keriann,
- **Karlene**, see Carlene
- **Kateena,** Katina,
- **Kaila**, Kailah, Kailla,
- **Kathereen**, Katherin,
- **Keith**, Keath, Origin: Scottish, Meaning: From the Place of Battle, Brave
- **Kirstine**, Kirston, Kirstyn,
- **Kerry**, Kearie, Keary,
- **Kellee**, Kelley, Kelli,

- ➢ **Kelsy**, Origin: Old Norse, Meaning: From Ship Island, Malleable
- ➢ **Kortney**, see Courtney
- ➢ **Kristall**, Kristalyn,
- ➢ **Kelsey**, Kelcea, Kelcee,
- ➢ **Kristine**, Kristeen,
- ➢ **Kate**, Cait, Cate, Kait, Origin: English, Meaning: Innocent, Godly Example
- ➢ **Keelee,** Keeleigh, Keelie,
- ➢ **Katareena**, Katerina,
- ➢ **Keila**, Kaela
- ➢ **Karlina,** see Carlina
- ➢ **Kellia,** Kelliana, Kellie, Origin: Irish, Meaning: Little Friend, Selfless
- ➢ **Kale**, Kayle, Origin: Hawaiian, Meaning: Farmer, Sower of Truth
- ➢ **Karylin,** Karylynn,
- ➢ **Kiernan**, Kieron, Origin: Irish, Meaning: Little, Blessed
- ➢ **Karlin,** Karlee see Carlin
- ➢ **Kristel**, Kristelle, Krystall,
- ➢ **Kristian**, Christian
- ➢ **Kylie,** Kylee, Kyleigh,

- **Kelissa,** Origin: English, Meaning: Fighter, Witness
- **Kelcey,** Kelcie, Kelcy,
- **Keena**, Kina, Origin: Irish, Meaning: Brave, Given Strength
- **Kelby**, Kelbee, Kelbey,
- **Kathryn**,
- **Kanika,** Kanicka,
- **Kateland**, Katclin,
- **Kali**, Kalli, Origin: Hawaiian, Meaning: Wreath of Flowers, Adorned
- **Karen**, Origin: Scandinavian, Meaning: Unblemished, Righteous
- **Kaitlin**, Kaetlin,
- **Kemp,** Khemp, Origin: English, Meaning: Champion, Zealous
- **Kyla,** Kylah, Kylla, Kyllah
- **Karlana,** see Carlana
- **Koren**, Coren, Corren,
- **Kobi**, Coby
- **Karl,** see Carl
- **Karalynn**, Karilyn,
- **Kari,** Karee, Karie, Karri
- **Kyie,** Origin: Bulgarian, Meaning: Throne, Temple of God

- **Karyna,** Karynna,
- **Karalie**, Origin: English, Meaning: Innocent, Righteous
- **Kenedy**, Kennady, Origin: Irish, Meaning: Ugly-Headed, Obedient
- **Kaylee**, Kaeleah,
- **Kellon**, Kellyn see also
- **Karla**, see Carla
- **Kelsee,** Kelsi, Kelsie,
- **Kallelgh,** Kailey, Kalee,
- **Kristina,** Khristina,
- **Karolyn**, Karalyn,
- **Karriana,**
- **Kaila,** Kayla, Origin: Middle Eastern, Meaning: Cherished Adored
- **Karilynn**, Kariln,
- **Kathlynn,** Katleen,
- **Keianna**, Kayana,
- **Karina,** Karine, Karinna,
- **Kaliana**, see Kaulana
- **Keilani**, Keilana,
- **Keenan**, Keanan,
- **Kellby**, Origin: Old German, Meaning: From the Spring Farm, Petition

- **Karlissa**, see Carlissa
- **Kisa**, Keesa, Keeson,
- **Karlynn**, Karlyn, Origin: Slavic, Meaning: Womanly, Valuable
- **Kaori**, Kaory, Origin: Japanese, Meaning: Strong, Majestic
- **Kalianna**, Origin: Hawaiian, Meaning: Famous, Strength of God
- **Karon**, Karren, Karron,
- **Katya**, Cata, Catia,
- **Kathleen**, Katheleen,
- **Kimberley,** Kimberli,
- **Kalea,** Kahlea, Kahleah,
- **Kirsten**, Keirstan,
- **Karmen**, see Carmen
- **Kannen**, Kanon
- **Kia,** Kiah, Origin: Nigerian, Meaning: Beginning of the Season, Sign
- **Kaileen**, Kaylene, Origin: Middle Eastern, Meaning: Sweetheart, Beloved
- **Kody**, Cody
- **Karina**, Origin: Norwegian, Meaning: Spotless, Purchased
- **Kaarianna**
- **Kinslea**, Kinsleigh,

- **Kimberlee,** Kimberleigh,
- **Kiley**, Kilee, Kileigh, Origin: Irish, Meaning: Attractive, Desirable
- **Kelly,** Kelia, Keli,
- **Kyle**, Kile, Kylan, Kylan,
- **Kristen**, Kristan, Kristi,
- **Keita**, Keeta, Origin: Scottish, Meaning: Enclosed Place, Joyful
- **Kato,** Katón
- **Karln,** Kaarin, Kárin,
- **Keelan,** Kealyn, Keelen,
- **Kristeena**, Krysteena,
- **Karen,** Kaaren, Karan,
- **Kariann,** Karianna,
- **Karalee**, Karalea,
- **Kristilynn**, Krystalin,
- **Kallan**, Kallen, Kallin,
- **Kinslee**, Origin: Old English, Meaning: Relative, Protected
- **Kelvin**, Kelvan, Kelvyn, Origin: Celtic, Meaning: From the Narrow River, Reasonable
- **Katherine**, Katharin,
- **Katrina**, Catarina,
- **Kylen,** Kylyn (see also

- **Kannon,** Kanen,
- **Krisstal,** Kristal, Kristalee,
- **Kadie,** Kady, Kaydee,
- **Karriem**, Origin: Middle Eastern, Meaning: Distinguished, Chosen
- **Kassandra**,
- **Killian**, Kilian, Origin: Irish, Meaning: Little Warrior, Attentive
- **Keliana,** Kelianna,
- **Kassidy**, Cassidy
- **Keira**, Keirra, Kera
- **Kimber,** Kimberlea,
- **Klaus,** Claas, Claus,
- **Kaley,** see Kaylee
- **Katelyn**, Katlyn, Kaytlin,
- **Kiesha**, Kisha (see also
- **Karena,** Kareena,
- **Keely**, Keilee, Kieley, Origin: Gaelic, Meaning: Beautiful, Trusting
- **Kanya,** Kania, Kanyah, Origin: Thai, Meaning: Young Lady, Prosperous
- **Katie,** Kaytee, Kaytie,
- **Kaitlinn**, Kaitlyn, Kaitlynn,
- **Kellsea**, Kellsee, Kellsie,
- **Kristene**, Krystine,

- **Kylen,** Kyler, Origin: Gaelic, Meaning: From the Strait Perceptive, Insight
- **Kiana,** Keanna, Keiana,
- **Kalin,** Kalyn, see Kaylyn
- **Kristie,** Kristii, Kristin,

L

- **Lezlee**, Lezley, Lezlie, Origin: Scottish, Meaning: From the Low Meadow, Remembered
- **Levina**, Leveena, Origin: Latin, Meaning: Flash of Lightning, Ardent Praise
- **Leonore**, Leonora,
- **Lindel**, Lyndel, Lyndell, Origin: Anglo-Saxon,
- **Lauren**, Lauran,
- **Liberty,** Libertee, Origin: Latin, Meaning: Freedom, Unchained
- **Lonny**, Origin: English, Meaning: Ready for Battle, God's Soldier
- **Lorence**, Lorentz,
- **Levona**, Livona, Origin: Hebrew, Meaning: Incense, Sacrifice
- **Leonard**, Len, Lenard,
- **Liona**, Origin: Latin, Meaning: Lioness, Courageous Spirit
- **Lance**, Lantz, Launce, Origin: German, Meaning: From the Land, Witness

- **Lydia**, Lidi, Lidia, Lidiya, Origin: Greek, Meaning: Womanly, Beautiful Light
- **Lonie**, Origin: German, Meaning: Lioness, Courageous
- **Larissa**, Larisa, Laryssa, Origin: Greek, Meaning: Cheerful, Grateful
- **Leandra**, Leandrea,
- **Leala,** Lealia, Leial,
- **Laine,** Laina, Lainee,
- **Langley**, Langsdon, Origin: Old English, Meaning: From the Long, Meadow Peaceful
- **Lacie**, Lacy, Origin: Latin, Meaning: Joyful, Filled With Praise
- **Lanae**, Lanai, Lanay,
- **Lora**, Laura
- **Lonnie**, Lon, Lonn,
- **Linda,** Linnea, Linnie,
- **Lyle,** Lisle, Lysle, Origin: Old French, Meaning: From the Island, Joyous Spirit
- **Lanny**, see Lawrence
- **Lori**, Origin: Latin, Meaning: Crowned With Honor, Victorious
- **Lionel**, Lional, Lionell,

- **Luanne**, Origin: Hebrew, Meaning: Graceful Warrior, Righteous
- **Lana**, Lanna, Lannah, Origin: Irish, Meaning: Attractive, Peaceful
- **Lando**, Landro, Origin: Portuguese, Meaning: From the Famous Land, Destined
- **Lena,** Leena, Lenah,
- **Leyland,** Origin: English, Meaning: From the Meadowland, Prosperous
- **Lindsy**, Lindzee, Linsay,
- **Lenny,** Leno, Léonard,
- **Laylee**, Laylie
- **Loren**, Larian, Larien,
- **Lada**, Ladah, Origin: Russian, Meaning: Beauty, Useful
- **Lincoln**, Lincon, Origin: Old English, Meaning: From the Pool Town, Victorious
- **Ladonna**, Ladona, La
- **Lauriane,** Laurianna,
- **Leona**, Leone, Leonia,
- **Leonardo**, Origin: Old German, Meaning: Strong as a Lion, Fearless Spirit
- **Laveda**, Lavedia, Origin: Latin, Meaning: Purified, Blessed

- **Liora**, Leora, Origin: Hebrew, Meaning: Glowing Light, Brilliance
- **Leonorah**, Origin: English, Meaning: Bright Like the Sun, Reflection of Christ
- **Lowell**, Lovell, Lowel, Origin: Latin, Meaning: Little Wolf, Peaceful
- **Lauri,** Laurie, Loree,
- **Lainey**, Origin: French, Meaning: Brilliant, Righteous
- **Lian**, Liane, Lianne
- **Lloyd**, Loyd, Origin: Welsh, Meaning: Wise, Seeker of Holiness
- **Lindsee**, Lindsi, Lindsie,
- **Lawrence**, Lanny,
- **Lyndon**, Lindan, Linden,
- **Lonna**, Lona, Loni,
- **Larry**, Lawrence
- **Laurell**, Origin: Latin, Laurel, Meaning: Faithful
- **Leah**, Lia, Liya, Origin: American, Meaning: Meadow, Guided of God
- **Leanoer,** Lenora, Lenore,
- **Lang,** Lange, Origin: Old Norse, Meaning: Tall, Lifted Up

- **Lisette,** Lissette, Origin: French, Meaning: Promise of God, One With Christ
- **Linsey**, Linsi, Linsie,
- **Lindee,** Lindey, Lindi,
- **Lynell**, Lynell, Lynnelle, Origin: English, Meaning: Pretty Virtuous
- **Liliana,** Liliane, Liljana,
- **Liana,** Leana, Leanna,
- **Luciann,** Lucie, Lucienne,
- **Linus,** Linas, Origin: Greek, Meaning: Fair-Haired, Treasurer of Wisdom and Knowledge
- **Landry**, Landré, Origin: French, Meaning: Ruler, Subject of God
- **Liedon**, Origin: Hebrew, Meaning: Justice is Mine, Defended
- **Louise**, Louisa, Luisa,
- **Lindon**, Lynden, Origin: English, Meaning: From the Lime Tree Hill, Excellent Worth
- **Levya**, Livie, Liviya, Livy,
- **Lindie**, Lindy, Origin: American, Meaning: Lovely, Witness
- **Loman**, Lomán, Origin: Serbian, Meaning: Delicate, Loving
- **Leora**, Liora

- **Leo**, Léo, Origin: Latin, Meaning: Lionhearted, Courageous
- **Louis,** Lou, Louie, Luigi,
- **Leia,** (see also Leigh, Lia,
- **Landon**, Landan, Landin, Origin: Old English, Meaning: From the Grassy Meadow, Comforted
- **Laurie**, see Lori
- **Lin**, Linh, Linn
- **Lilliana**, Lillianna,
- **Lawton**, Laughton, Origin: English, Meaning: From the Hill Town, Seeker of Truth
- **Leanna,** see Liana
- **Lila,** Origin: Hebrew, Meaning: Dark Beauty, Bringer of Light
- **Lindsey**, Lindsay,
- **Linzey**, Lynnzey, Lynsay,
- **Leann**, Leann, Leanne,
- **Libby**, Libbee, Libbey,
- **LeRoy**, Origin: Old French, Meaning: Royal, Esteemed
- **Larry**, Laurence, Laurens,
- **Lenore**, Leanore
- **Lillian**, Lilli, Lilia, Lilian,
- **Lynsee**, Lynsey, Lynzey,

- **Levia**, Levya, Origin: Hebrew, Meaning: Attached, One With God
- **Laura,** Origin: Latin, Meaning: Famous God's Gracious, Gift
- **Laela**, Layla
- **Lewis**, Lew, Lewie, Origin: Old English, Meaning: Safeguard of the People, Righteous
- **Leila,** Laila, Leala, Lelea
- **Leandria**, Leandra, Origin: English, Meaning: Brave as a Lion, Steadfast
- **Lexi,** Leksa, Lexa,
- **Lynelle**, Linell, Linnell,
- **Leon**, Léon, Leone, Origin: English, Meaning: Brave as a Lion, Brave
- **Liezel**, Liezl, Lisel, Origin: German, Meaning: Oath of God, Promise
- **Lorrie**, (see also Laura), Origin: English, Meaning: Crowned With Honor, Hopeful
- **Logan**, Logen, Origin: Celtic, Meaning: From the Little Hollow, Devoted to God
- **Libbie**, Origin: English, Meaning: Promise of God, Preserved
- **Lahela**, Lahaela, Lahaila, Origin: Hawaiian, Meaning: Lamb, Redeemed
- **Lars**, Larsen, Larson,

- ➢ **Lennox**, Lenox, Origin: Scottish, Meaning: Placid Stream, God is All-Sufficient
- ➢ **Lexey**, Lexee, Lexia,
- ➢ **Levi**, Leevi, Levey, Levy, Origin: Hebrew, Meaning: Harmonious, Enlightened
- ➢ **Ludwig**, Ludvig, Origin: German, Meaning: Famous Warrior, Gifted
- ➢ **Leah,** Lea, Léa, Leeah,
- ➢ **Lancelot,** Launcelot, Origin: Old French, Meaning: Attendant God's Helper
- ➢ **Locke,** Lock, Origin: Old English, Meaning: From the Forest, Wise
- ➢ **Lex,** Lexx, Origin: English, Meaning: Defender of Mankind, Protector
- ➢ **Lola,** Lolita, Origin: Latin, Meaning: Owned With Compassion and Grace, Perceptive Insight
- ➢ **Lemond,** Origin: French, Meaning: From the Earth, Blessed
- ➢ **Luis,** Origin: Old German, Meaning: Famous Warrior, Declarer of God
- ➢ **Lia**, Liah
- ➢ **Lynda**, Origin: Spanish, Meaning: Beautiful, Excellent Virtue

- **Lilith,** Lillith, Origin: Hebrew, Meaning: Night Owl, Wise
- **Lamont**, Lamonte,
- **Lillyann**, Lily, Origin: Latin, Meaning: Purity, Shining Light
- **Lina,** Origin: Greek, Meaning: Gentle, Blessed Peacemaker
- **Luann**, Luana, Luanna,
- **Lane**, Laney, Lanie,
- **Laurel**, Laural, Laurall,
- **Lois**, Origin: Greek, Meaning: Desired, Established in Truth
- **London**, Londan,
- **Liesel,** Leisel, Liesel,
- **Lida,** Leeda, Lita, Origin: Meaning: Slavic, Love, Beloved
- **Lander,** Landers, Origin: Basque, Meaning: Like a Lion, Powerful
- **Lisanne**, Lise
- **Layla,** Laela, Laylah,
- **Lisa,** Leesa, Liesa, Liisa,
- **Langston,** Langsdon, Origin: Old English, Meaning: From the Tall Man's Town, Rescued

M

- **Miron**, Miran
- **Maxwell**, Max, Maxx, Origin: Scottish, Meaning: From the Great Spring, Righteous
- **Marian**, Mariana,
- **Milan**, Milon, Mylan,
- **Meggie**, Meghan,
- **Malorie**, Malory, Origin: German, Meaning: Counselor, Joyful
- **Madalaina**, Madaline,
- **Meg**, Megan, Megen,
- **Martin,** Martan, Marten,
- **Megan**, Maegan,
- **Mindie**, Myndee, Myndie, Origin: English, Meaning: Sweet as Honey, Genuine
- **Marrissia,** Marysa,
- **Mischel,** Mishayle,
- **Mayo**, Maiyo, Origin: Irish, Meaning: From the Yew-Tree, Plain Heart of Praise

- **Marilu**, Marilow, Marylou, Origin: American, Meaning: Bitter Grace, Blessed
- **Manleigh**, Origin: Irish, Meaning: Heroic, Victorious Spirit
- **Macdonald**, McDonald,
- **Mallory**, Mallari, Mallary,
- **Mélissa**, Mellisa,
- **Monica,** Moneka, Moni,
- **Malcolm**, Malcom, Origin: Scottish, Meaning: Diligent Servant, Teachable Spirit
- **Mannuel**, Manny
- **Medina**, Medaena,
- **Miron**, Origin: Greek, Meaning: Fragrant Ointment, Peaceful Praise
- **Melanie**, Melanie,
- **Milo**, Mylo, Origin: Old German, Meaning: Generous, Helpful Spirit
- **McKinnley**, Origin: Irish, Meaning: Child of the Scholarly Ruler, Peaceful
- **Malerie**, Mallerie,
- **Maris**, Marisa, Marise,
- **Mercedes**, Mersade, Origin: Latin, Meaning: Gift, Esteemed
- **Mathilda**, Tilda, Tillie, Origin: German, Meaning: Noble Lady, Beloved

- **Magdelina**, Magdeline,
- **Misha,** Mischa, Mishka, Origin: Russian, Meaning: Who Is Like God? Disciple
- **Molly**, Mollee, Molley,
- **Marlon**, Marlin, Origin: Welsh, Meaning: From the Hill by the Sea, Victorious Spirit
- **Margeret**, Margerite,
- **Murray**, Murrey, Origin: Gaelic, Meaning: Sailor, Discerning
- **Marly**, Marlys, Marlysa,
- **Macy**, Macee, Macey,
- **Marthina**, Martinia,
- **Mona**, Monna, Moyna, Origin: Irish, Meaning: Noble, Reflection of Wisdom
- **Magdalina**, Magdaline,
- **Milana**, Milanna, Milania
- **Milian**
- **Michaele**, Michaelle,
- **Mariele**, Mariella,
- **Michala**, Michayle,
- **Milana,** Milena, Origin: Hebrew, Meaning: Tower, Secure
- **Morris**, Maurice

- **Manning**, Maning, Origin: English, Meaning: Child of the Her,o Obedient
- **Mark,** Marc, Marciano,
- **McGwire**, Origin: Irish, Meaning: Child of the Fair One, Trustworthy
- **Maggie**, Maggee, Maggi, Origin: Greek, Meaning: Pearl Of Great, Value
- **Madlen**, Madlin,
- **Mingan,** Mingen, Origin: Native American, Meaning: Gray Wolf, Vigilant
- **Madonna,** Madona, Origin: Latin, Meaning: My Lady, Pure
- **Meagann**, Meagen,
- **Michael**, Mekhail,
- **Mendel**, Mendell, Origin: Hebrew, Meaning: Wisdom, Studious
- **Marylou**, Marilu
- **Melvin**, Malvin, Mel, Origin: Middle English, Meaning: Reliable Friend, Excellent Virtue
- **Milton,** Milt, Mylton, Origin: English, Meaning: From the Mill Town Blessed of God
- **Medora**, Medorra, Origin: English, Meaning: Mother's Gift, Blessing
- **Madisson**, Origin: Old English, Meaning: Child of the Valiant Warrior, Brave

- **Mindy**, Mindee, Mindi,
- **Mavis**, Mayvis, Origin: French, Meaning: Songbird, Praise
- **Marina**, Marena,
- **Murphy**, Murfey, Origin: Irish, Meaning: Sea Warrior, Full of Praise
- **Manley**, Manlea,
- **Magdelena,** Magdelene,
- **Molli,** Mollie, Origin: English, Meaning: Desired, Righteous
- **Marsden**, Marsdon, Origin: English, Meaning: From the Boundary Valley, Preserved
- **Magnus**, Magnes, Origin: Latin, Meaning: Great, Privileged
- **Martinez**, Marton, Marty,
- **Mauriell,** Maurielle
- **Manon,** Mannon, Origin: French, Meaning: Wished-for, Fulfilled
- **Maynard**, Ménard, Origin: Old English, Meaning: Powerful, Spirit of Praise
- **Mathew**, Mathias,
- **Merlin**, Merle, Merlen, Origin: Old English, Meaning: Falcon, Courageous
- **Malin**, Mallin, Mallon,

- **Marie**, Maree (see also
- **Mike**, Mikhael, Mikhail,
- **Marsha**, Marsi, Marsi,
- **Mina**, Mini, Minni,
- **Merissa**, Origin: English, Meaning: Bitterness, Eternally Steadfast
- **McArthur**, Origin: Scottish, Meaning: Child of the Brave, Forgiven
- **Millissa**, Missi, Missie,
- **Mario**, Marios, Marrio, Origin: Italian, Meaning: Sailor, Regenerated
- **Marika,** Marica, Marrika,
- **Marino**, Origin: Latin, Meaning: Warlike, Powerful
- **Martrina**, Martyna, Origin: Hispanic, Meaning: Lady of the House, Virtuous
- **Michah**, Mycah, Origin: Hebrew, Meaning: Who Is Like God? Reverent
- **Minnie,** Minny, Origin: Old German, Meaning: Love, Cherished
- **Myla,** Mylah, Mylea,
- **Maayan**, Maayana,
- **Miki**, Mikki, Mychal,
- **Manuel**, Manni,
- **Marianna**, Marianne,

- **Mariane**, Mariann,
- **Maximillian**, Max, Maxx, Origin: Latin, Meaning: Greatest in Excellence, Teachable Spirit
- **May,** Mae, Maye, Origin: Hebrew, Meaning: Gift of God, Blessed
- **Maya**, Mayah
- **Maria**, Marea, Mareah,
- **McKenzee**, McKenzie, Origin: Gaelic, Meaning: Child of the Wise Leader, Witness
- **Madoline**, Origin: Greek, Meaning: Magnificent, Prayerful
- **Melissa**, Malissa,
- **Mildred**, Midge, Mildrid, Origin: Old English, Meaning: Gentle Spirit, Loving Spirit
- **Marylin**, Origin: English, Meaning: Bitterness, Sacrifice of Praise
- **Marion,** Marian
- **Melani**, Mélanie,
- **Mervin,** Marvin
- **Marsello**, Origin: Latin, Meaning: Industrious Worker, Strong in Spirit
- **Martiza**, Martoya,
- **Mali**, Malee, Maley, Malí
- **Maryssa**, Meris, Merisa,

- **Menora**, Manora, Origin: Hebrew, Meaning: Candelabrum, Witness
- **Mylen,** Mylon, Origin: Italian, Meaning: From Milan Witness
- **Mikaela**, Mikalya, Mikyla,
- **Mariel**, Marial, Mariela,
- **Mimie**, Mimii, Origin: English, Meaning: Wished-for, Spiritual Passion
- **Mimi**, Mimee, Mimie,
- **Malia,** Maleah, Maleia,
- **Maylin**, Origin: Old English, Meaning: Little Warrior, Champion
- **Marilynn**, Marralin,
- **Mellicent**, Millee, Millie,
- **Martina**, Martel, Martelle,
- **Michal,** Machelle,
- **Mustafa**, Mostafa,
- **Maci,** Macie, Origin: French, Meaning: From the Matthew's Estate, Enlightened
- **Magdalyn**, Magdelana,
- **Matthew**, Mateo,
- **Marcellus**, Marsel,
- **Mickey**, Mickie, Micky,
- **Martie**, Martika, Marty,
- **Mia**, Meah, Miah

- **Macia**, Macya, Origin: Polish, Meaning: Wished-for, Blameless
- **Marcia**, Marcee, Marci,
- **Merrall**, Merryl, Meryll
- **Meryl**, Meral, Merel,
- **Milly**, Origin: Old German, Meaning: Industrious, Strong Spirit

N

- ➤ **Nikolette**, Nikolle,
- ➤ **Nevan**, Neven, Nevin,
- ➤ **Nils,** Niels, Niles, Origin: Scandinavian, Meaning: Champion, Triumphant
- ➤ **Nykolas**, Nikita, Origin: Greek, Meaning: Victory of the People, Triumphant Spirit
- ➤ **Norris**, Noris, Origin: Old English, Meaning: Northerner, Wise
- ➤ **Nealon**, Neile, Neill,
- ➤ **Nigel**, Niegel, Nigell,
- ➤ **Norma**, Noma, Origin: Latin, Meaning: Perfection, Model of Excellence
- ➤ **Normand**, Normen,
- ➤ **Nola,** Nuala, Origin: Latin, Meaning: Small Bell Harmonious
- ➤ **Norton**, Nortan, Origin: Middle English, Meaning: From the North Town, Integrity
- ➤ **Nevill**, Origin: Old French, Meaning: From the New Town, Compassionate Spirit
- ➤ **Noel**, Noél, Noël, Noela,

- **Natalie**, Natalea,
- **Newell**, Newall, Origin: Middle English, Meaning: From the New Hall, Sincere
- **Neva**, Neyva, Origin: English, Meaning: New, Obedient
- **Nerissa,** Narissa, Origin: English, Meaning: Sea Nymph, Expectant
- **Neriah**, Neri, Neria,
- **Neilon**, Origin: Irish, Meaning: Champion, Beloved
- **Nikolyn**, Niquole, Nykola,
- **Nixon**, Origin: English, Meaning: Son of the Victor, Overcomer
- **Nydia**, Origin: Slavic, Meaning: Hopeful, Blessed
- **Nadine**, Nadean,
- **Norman**, Norm,
- **Nikolai,** Nikolas,
- **Normie**, Origin: Old English, Meaning: Man From the North, Courageous Spirit
- **Nichalas**, Nicholas,
- **Nikolos**, Nycholas,
- **Nevon**, Navin, Origin: Irish, Meaning: Holy, Righteous
- **Neville**, Nevil, Nevile,

- **Newton**, Newtyn, Origin: Middle English, Meaning: From the New Town, Helpful Counselor
- **Neil,** Neal, Neale,
- **Nellie,** Nel, Nell, Nelle,
- **Nelson**, Neilson, Nelsen,
- **Nikolaus**, Nikolai, Nikoli,
- **Napoleon**, Origin: Greek, Meaning: Lion of the Woodland, Bold
- **Noella**, Noelle, Origin: Latin, Meaning: Christmas Child, Precious Gift
- **Noele,** Noelia, Noelle,
- **Nellee**, Nelley, Nelli, Origin: English, Meaning: Shining, Witness
- **Nancy**, Nan, Nana,
- **Nadia**, Origin: Latin, Meaning: Nest, Spiritual Potenial
- **Ninah**, Origin: English, Meaning: Grace of God, Delivered
- **Natasha**, natachia,

O

- **Oakley**, Oaklee,
- **Oscar**, Oskar, Origin: Old English, Meaning: Divine Spearman, Appointed of God
- **Odessa**, Odyssa, Origin: Greek, Meaning: Long Voyage, Preserved
- **Olivia**, Olive, Olivea,
- **Oprah**, Origin: Hebrew, Meaning: Runaway
- **Octavio**, Octavien,
- **Otto**, Oto, Origin: German, Meaning: Prosperous, Esteemed
- **Olga**, Olya, Origin: Scandinavian, Meaning: Holy, Wise
- **Oya**, Oiya, Origin: Miwok, Meaning: Called Forth Witness
- **Octavius**, Octavian,
- **Odysseua**, Odesseus, Origin: Greek, Meaning: Wrathful, Righteous
- **Osmond**, Osmund, Origin: Old English, Meaning: Divine Protector, God's Warrior

- **Orlando**, Orlanda,
- **Otis**, Ottis, Origin: Greek, Meaning: Keen of Hearing, Open to Divine Inspiration
- **Oswald**, Osvaldo,
- **Orlondo**, Origin: Italian, Meaning: Famous Throughout the Land, Renowned
- **Owen**, Owens, Origin: Greek, Meaning: Distinguished, Pleasant to Look Upon
- **Ozzie**, Origin: Hebrew, Meaning: Courage, Overcomer
- **Octavious**, Origin: Latin, Meaning: Eighth, Abiding in God
- **Orion**, Orien, Origin: Greek, Meaning: Son of Fire, Zealous
- **Orli**, Ori, Orlie, Origin: Hebrew, Meaning: My Light, Fearless
- **Odell**, Odie, Origin: Middle English, Meaning: From the Wooded Hill, Hopeful
- **Odella**, Odeleya, Origin: Hebrew, Meaning: I Will Praise God, Thankful Spirit
- **Orin**, Origin: Hebrew, Meaning: Ash Tree, Blessed
- **Oliver**, Olley, Ollie,
- **Orpah**, Ophra, Opra,

➢ **Oxford**, Oxforde, Origin: Old English, Meaning:
The Place Where the Oxen Cross the Restful

P

- **Paul**, Pasha, Pauley,
- **Pauli**, Paulis, Paolo,
- **Pilar**, Pillar, Origin: Latin, Meaning: Pillar, Strong in Faith
- **Preston**, Prestan, Origin: Old English, Meaning: From the Priest's Home, Consecrated to God
- **Phoebe,** see Phebe
- **Pete,** Péter, Petr, Petey,
- **Phyllis**, Phylliss, Origin: Greek, Meaning: Green Branch, Youthful Trust
- **Pia,** Piya, Origin: Italian, Meaning: Devoted, Focused
- **Palmer**, Palmar, Origin: Old English, Meaning: Peaceful, Pilgrim Bringer of Peace
- **Porter**, Port, Origin: Latin, Meaning: Gatekeeper, Watchful Spirit
- **Pamela,** Pam, Pamala,
- **Pervis**, Purvis, Origin: Latin, Meaning: Passage, Messenger

- **Price**, Pryce, Origin: Welsh, Meaning: Son of the Ardent One, Eager
- **Philipp**, Philippe, Phill,
- **Peggy,** Peg, Pegg, Peggi, Origin: English, Meaning: Pearl Promise
- **Phylicia**, see Felecia
- **Peli,** Pelí, Basque, Happy, Filled With Joy
- **Penelope,** Pennelope,
- **Pricilla,** Priscila, Prisilla,
- **Patience,** Paishence, Origin: English, Meaning: Endurance, Fortunate, Firmness of Spirit
- **Pauline,** Paulla, Origin: Latin, Meaning: Small Loving
- **Parker**, Parkker, Origin: Middle English, Meaning: Guardian of the Park, Spiritual Light
- **Paris**, Parras, Parris, Origin: Greek, Meaning: Attractive, Godly
- **Pablo**, Paublo, Origin: Spanish, Meaning: Small Bell, Great Faith
- **Paula**, Paula, Paolina,
- **Payne**, Paine, Origin: Latin, Meaning: From the Country, Sacred
- **Pierce,** Pearce, Peerce,

- **Presley**, Presleigh, Origin: Old English, Meaning: From the Priest's Meadow, Peaceful Spirit
- **Paulo**, Paulus, Pavel, Origin: Latin, Meaning: Small, Dynamo of Energy and Faith
- **Pele,** Pelé, Peleh, Origin: Hebrew, Meaning: Miracle, Strong Faith
- **Peter**, Peder, Petar,
- **Peyton**, Paiton, Payden,
- **Park**, Parke, Origin: Chinese, Meaning: Cyprus Tree, Blessed
- **Phebe,** Phoebe, Origin: Greek, Meaning: Bright, Cherished
- **Parnell,** Parnel, Pernell, Origin: French, Meaning: Little Peter, Faithfulness
- **Perry**, Parry
- **Paxton**, Paxon, Paxten, Origin: Old English, Meaning: From the Peaceful Town, Prepared
- **Paulette,** Paulina,
- **Piper,** Origin: English, Meaning: Pipe Player, Joyous Spirit
- **Petra**, Petrina, Pietra, Origin: Greek, Meaning: Small Rock, Strong and Everlasting
- **Peirce**, Origin: English, Meaning: Stone, Strong in Spirit

➤ **Piran**, Pieran, Origin: Irish, Meaning: Prayer, Supplicant

Q

- **Quinn,** Quin, Origin: Gaelic, Meaning: Intelligent, Godly Insight
- **Quimby**, Quinby, Origin: Scandinavian, Meaning: From the Queen's Estate, Vigilant Spirit
- **Quintana**, Quinta,
- **Quincy,** Quincey, Quinci,
- **Quenby,** Quenbie, Origin: Swedish, Meaning: Feminine, Holy
- **Quinton,** Quintus,

R

- **Rebeca**, Rébecca,

- **Reggie**, Regi, Regie,

- **Reeve**, Reaves, Reeves, Origin: Middle English, Meaning: Steward, Servant

- **Raechel**, Raechele,

- **Ranee**, Rania

- **Rosalin**, Rosalina,

- **Rollie**, Rowland, Origin: Old German, Meaning: Famous Throughout the Land, Full of Wisdom

- **Richards**, Richie, Rick,

- **Randi**, Randalin,

- **Raina**, Raenah, Rainna

- **Royce**, Roice, Origin: Old English, Meaning: Son of the King, Tranquil Spirit

- **Roanna**, Origin: Indo-Pakistani, Meaning: Stringed Instrument, Joyful Praise

- **Roxane,** Roxann, Roxi,

- **Ralph,** Ralf

- **Rose Anne**,

- **Raelynn**, Rayele,

- **Rossanna,** Rozana,

- **Reagan**, Reaganne,

- **Rhiauna,** Rhyan,

- **Rodrik,** Rodrique,

- **Ruben**, Rubin, Origin: Hebrew, Meaning: Behold, A Son Wondrous Recognition

- **Rosamond**, Rosamund, Origin: Old German, Meaning: Guardian Protector of Truth

- **Rogan**, Rogann, Origin: Irish, Meaning: Redhead, Persevering

- **Reba,** Reva, Rheba, Origin: English, Meaning: Bound, Witness

- **Rune,** Roone, Origin: Swedish, Meaning: Secret, Guarded of God

- **Ricquie**, Rik, Riki, Rikk,

- **Rosannah**, Rosangela,

- **Rachaele,** Rachal,

- **Reginia,** Reginna, Origin: Latin, Meaning: Queen, Gracious

- **Rylee**, Rylie, Origin: Irish, Meaning: Valiant, Protected

- **Rea,** Reah, Reha (see

- **Richmond**, Richmon, Origin: French, Meaning: From the Hill of Wealthy, Vegetati Nourished

- **Raelina,** Raelle, Raelyn,

- **Rodney,** Rod, Rhodney,

- **Roseannah**, Rossana,

- **Raphael**, Raphaela

- **Rubi,** Rubie, Origin: French, Meaning: Beautiful Jewel, Full of Grace

- **Rachel**, Rachael,

- **Rozalyn,** Rozalyn,

- **Rex,** Rexx, Origin: Latin, Meaning: King, Leadership

- **Rickey**, Ricki, Rickie,

- **Ranie**, Origin: Hebrew, Meaning: My Song, Praise

- **Reese**, Reece, Rhys, Origin: Welsh, Meaning: Enthusiastic, Dedicated

- **Rose**, Rosa, Rosey,

- **Robert**, Bob, Bobb,

- **Roger,** Rodger, Rog,

- **Robertson,** Robinson,

- **Rosalinda**, Rosalyn,

- **Rhea,** Rhaya, Rhéa,

- **Roxie,** Roxy, Origin: Persian, Meaning: Sunrise, Heavenly

- **Randoph**, Randolf, Origin: Old English, Meaning: Shield, Established in Peace

- **Ranios,** Origin: Old German, Meaning: Mighty Army, Strength of God

- **Rachele,** Racquel,

- **Rufus,** Ruffus, Origin: Latin, Meaning: Red-Haired, Excellent Virtue

- **Reginald,** Reg, Reggie,

- **Roy,** Roi, Origin: French, Meaning: King, Seeker of Wisdom

- **Ranger,** Rainger, Range, Origin: French, Meaning: Keeper of the Forest, Covenant

- **Rudolph,** Rudi, Rudy, Origin: Old German, Meaning: Great and Famous, Resourceful

- **Reid,** Raed, Reade,

- **Rowena**, Rowina, Origin: Welsh, Meaning: Peaceful, Wise

- **Ronia**, Ronnee, Ronney,

- **Rosi**, Rosie, Rosy, Roza,

- **Roseanna**, Rosana,

- **Ranon**, Ranen, Rani,

- **Roberta,** Birdee, Birdie,

- **Reynald**, Reynaldo,

- **Rainor,** Rainar, Rainer,

- **Roseann**, Rose Ann,

- **Richele,** Richella (see

- **Rachelle**, Rochelle

- **Rolland,** Rollando, Rolle,

- **Regis,** Reggis, Origin: Latin, Meaning: Regal, Honored

- **Randie**, Randie, Randii, Origin: English, Meaning: Shield, Guarded

- **Rowen,** Rowan, Origin: Irish, Meaning: Red, Purchased

- **Rhodes,** Rhoads, Origin: Greek, Meaning: From the Island of Roses, Formed of God

- **Reesa,** Resa, Reesha,

- **Rebecca**, Rabecca,

- **Ross**, Roess, Origin: Gaelic, Meaning: Knight, Victorious

- **Rosine,** Rosina, Origin: Italian, Meaning: Cherished, Bold

- **Ruby**, Rubia, Rubey,

- **Roxanne**, Roxana,

- **Russell,** Russ, Russel,

- **René,** Raeneé, Rainato,

- **Radleigh**, Origin: English, Meaning: From the Reed Meadow, Spirit-Filled

- **Robyn**, Robynn, Origin: English, Meaning: Shining Fame, Victorious Spirit

- **Raanan**, Ranaan, Ranan

- **Reena**, Rena

- **Robin,** Robbin, Robbyn,

- **Regina,** Regeena, Reggi,

- **Renée,** Origin: French, Meaning: Born Again, Joyful

- **Raechell**, Raeschelle,

- **Ronni,** Ronee, Roni,

- **Rosalynn,** Roselynn,

- **Rodrigo**, Rodriguez,

- **Richelle,** Richela,

- **Rozalie,** Rozalin,

- **Reiko,** Reyko, Origin: Japanese, Meaning: Sign, Miraculous

- **Roza,** Rozee, Rozy, Origin: Latin, Meaning: Rose, God's Gracious Gift

- **Regan**, Raegan,

- **Rodnee**, Origin: Anglo-Saxon, Meaning: From the Clearing on the Island, Joyful

- **Raelene,** Raeleen,

- **Rozália,** Rozalee,

- **Richard,** Ric, Ricardo,

- **Reyanna,** Reyanne,

- **Remi,** Remee, Rémi,

- **Ricky,** Rico, Ricqui,

- **Reubin,** Rheuben,

- **Roberto,** Roberts,

- **Randy**, Ranndy, Origin: English, Meaning: Shield, Protected

- **Rhoda,** Rhodi, Rhody, Origin: Greek, Meaning: From the Island of Roses, God's Unfolded Love

- **Ronnie,** Ronny, Ronya, Origin: English, Meaning: Power, Strength

- **Ramón,** Ramone

S

- **Silas,** Sylas, Origin: Latin, Meaning: From the Forest, Steadfast in Trust

- **Sammie**, Sammuel,

- **Sylvia**, Silva, Silvana,

- **Sanders**, Sander,

- **Silvia**, Sylvia

- **Shanna**, Shannah,

- **Sven**, Svein, Swen, Origin: Scandinavian, Meaning: Youth, Loving

- **Sandee**, Sandi, Sandie,

- **Sahara**, Saharah, Origin: English, Meaning: Wilderness, Strengthened

- **Selby**, Selbey, Origin: English, Meaning: From the Mansion, Child of God

- **Sabrina**, Sabreena,

- **Sebastian**, Sabastien,

- **Seeley**, see Ceeley

- **Salli**, Sallie, Origin: Old English, Meaning: Princess, Beloved

- **Shana,** Shanae,

- **Sadee**, Saydee, Origin: English, Meaning: Princess, Beautiful

- **Sydney**, Sidney

- **Skylar**, Skylee, Sklie,

- **Sheliah**, Shiela, Shyla, Origin: English, Meaning: Blind, Wise

- **Sullivan**, Sulley, Sullie,

- **Sean**, Séan, Seán,

- **Suzie**, Suzy, Origin: Hebrew, Meaning: Graceful, Lily Purity

- **Sammy**, Samuele, Origin: Hebrew, Meaning: God Has Heard, Instructed of God

- **Sheldon**, Shelden,

- ➢ **Sapphira**, Safire, Saffire,

- ➢ **Selma**, Selmah, Zelma, Origin: Celtic, Meaning: Divinely Protected, Enlightened Spirit

- ➢ **Sylvester**, Silvester,

- ➢ **Salina**, Salena, Saleena

- ➢ **Scotty**, Origin: Old English, Meaning: From Scotland, Temple of God

- ➢ **Selam**, Saalam, Salaam,

- ➢ **Serenah**, Serrenna,

- ➢ **Selaam**, Origin: Ethiopian, Meaning: Peaceful, Content

- ➢ **Sahra**, Sahra, Sara,

- ➢ **Sanya**, Sania, Saniya, Origin: Indo-Pakistani, Meaning: Born on Saturday, Believer

- ➢ **Safron**, Saffrón, Origin: English, Meaning: Flower, Valuable Spice

- ➢ **Sapphire**, Origin: Greek, Meaning: Gem, Precious

- **Sebina**, Sebinah, Origin: Latin, Meaning: Planter of Vines, Spiritual Discernment

- **Simone**, Samona,

- **Sandy**, Saundra, Sondra,

- **Summer**, Origin: English, Meaning: Summer, Ordained

- **Sawyer**, Soiyer, Origin: English, Meaning: Wood Worker, Gifted

- **Sionna**, Origin: Hebrew, Meaning: Apex, Productive

- **Simon**, Shimon,

- **Sophia**, Sofi, Soffi,

- **Suzann**, Suzanna,

- **Scott,** Scot, Scottie,

- **Stacie**, Stacy, Stasia,

- **Sheila**, Sheela, Sheelah, Meaning: Beginning, Miraculous

- **Skelly**, Skelley, Origin: Gaelic, Meaning: Storyteller, Treasure of Knowledge

- ➤ **Sébastien**, Origin: Greek, Meaning: Venerable, Esteemed

- ➤ **Sydnee,** Sydney, Sydnie,

- ➤ **Skyelar**, Skyla, Skylah,

- ➤ **Sage**, Saige, Origin: English, Meaning: Wise, Discerning

- ➤ **Shauna**

- ➤ **Silvanna**, Silvia, Silvania,

- ➤ **Salvador**, Sal,

- ➤ **Sharai**, Sharaiah,

- ➤ **Shaina**, Shaena,

- ➤ **Skye**, Sky, Origin: Middle Eastern, Meaning: Supplier of Water, Miraculous Creation

- ➤ **Sandra**, Sahndra,

- ➤ **Summer**, Sommer

- ➤ **Skyler**, Schylar, Schyler,

- ➤ **Savana**, Savannah,

- ➤ **Selena**, Selenia, Selina,

- **Siona**, Siauna, Siaunna,

- **Sally**, Sallee, Salley,

- **Sadie**, S'ade, Sad'e,

- **Santiago**, Sántiago, Origin: Spanish, Meaning: Saint, Gifted

- **Sandrea**, Sandreea,

- **Selyna**, Sylena, Sylina,

- **Savanna**, Savauna,

- **Stacey**, Stacia, Stacee,

- **Shelby**, Shelbee,

- **Shawne**, Shawnn,

- **Sadhana**, Origin: Indo-Pakistani, Meaning: Devotion, Persistent

- **Stafanie**, Staffany,

- **Samuel**, Sam, Samm,

- **Susanna**, Susanne, Sue,

- **Skyllar**, Skyller, Skylor, Origin: Dutch, Meaning: Scholar, Wise

- **Serena**, Sarina, Sereena,

- **Suzanne**, Suzette, Suzi,

- **Simba**, Symba, Origin: Swahili, Meaning: Lion, Blessed

- **Sabina**, Sabinna,

- **Sandreia**, Sandira,

- **Saxon**, Sax, Saxen, Origin: Middle English, Meaning: Swordsman, Valorous

- **Sylvana**, Sylvanya,

- **Shelbey**, Shelbie, Shellby, Origin: Old English, Meaning: From the Estate on the Slope, Faithful Steward

- **Sarah,** Saara, Saarah,

T

- **Tala**, Tallah, Origin: Native American, Meaning: Stalking Wolf, Tamed
- **Talia**, Talaya, Talea,
- **Tobiah**, Tobie, Tobi,
- **Thomas**, Thom,
- **Trent**, Trente, Origin: English, Meaning: Rapid Stream, Renewed
- **Trinette**, Trinice,
- **Tereese,** Terese, Teresa,
- **Tyson**, Tison, Tyce,
- **Trey**, Trae, Trai, Origin: Middle English, Meaning: Third, Sacrifice
- **Troy**, Troi, Troye, Origin: Gaelic, Meaning: Foot Soldier, Steadfast
- **Terry** (see also Tarrant), Origin: Latin, Meaning: Tender, Gently Formed
- **Trenten**, Trentin, Origin: Old English,
- **Tria**, Triana, Trianna,
- **Tifnie**, Tifny, Tiphanee,

- **Timothé**, Timothée,
- **Trevor**, Trev, Trevar,
- **Timothi**, Tymothee,
- **Tia**, Téa, Teeya, Teia,
- **Trever**, Origin: Irish, Meaning: Prudent, Righteous
- **Trusten**, Trustan, Trustin
- **Tiana**, Teana, Teanna,
- **Tyra,** Tyraa, Tyrah,
- **Treysa**, Treyssa, Origin: Greek, Meaning: Harvester, Bountiful Spirit
- **Traecee,** Traecey,
- **Tucker**, Origin: Old English, Meaning: Folder of Cloth, Efficient
- **Tullis**, Tullias, Tullius, Origin: Latin, Meaning: Rank, Admirable
- **Talbot,** Talbott, Origin: Old German, Meaning: Bright Valley, Promise
- **Typhanee**, Typhany, Origin: English, Meaning: Divine Showing, Beloved
- **Theron**, Theran, Therron, Origin: Greek, Meaning: Hunter, Efficient
- **Trenton**, Trendon,
- **Tyshia**, (see also Taesha), Origin: English, Meaning: Joy, Thankful

- **Tristen**, Trista, Tristan,
- **Trina,** Treena, Treina,
- **Trilbie,** Origin: English, Meaning: Hat, Covered
- **Tracey**, Trace, Tracee,
- **Tania**, Tahnia, Tahniya,
- **Tristia**, Tristian, Tristiana,
- **Timothy**, Tim, Timmie,
- **Traicey**, Trasee, Trasey
- **Tiarra**, Tiárra, Tiera,
- **Tiara**, Tearra, Teira,
- **Tani**, Tahnee, Tahnie,
- **Thelma**, Thellma, Origin: Greek, Meaning: Willful, Strong in Spirit
- **Tiandra,** Tianika, Tilia, Origin: Spanish, Meaning: Aunt, Pure
- **Tyfanny**, Tyfanni, Tyffini,
- **Traci**, Tracia, Tracie,
- **Timmothy**, Timmy,
- **Theressa,** Thereza,
- **Tifaney**, Tifani, Tifanie,
- **Tianna,** Origin: Greek, Meaning: Princess, Praised
- **Tilden**, Tildan, Origin: Old English, Meaning: From the Blessed Valley, Peaceful Spirit

- **Taria**, Tarin, Taris,
- **Truman**, Trumann, Origin: English, Meaning: Honest Faithful
- **Thor**, Thorin, Origin: Old Norse, Meaning: Thunder, God's Warrior
- **Tal**, Talley, Tally, Origin: Hebrew, Meaning: Rain, Blessing
- **Tylor**, Origin: Middle English, Meaning: Tile Maker, Resourceful
- **Theresa**, Taresa, Tarisa,
- **Tyler**, Ty, Tylar, Tyller,
- **Tierney**, Tiernan, Origin: Irish, Meaning: Lordly, Gracious Spirit
- **Tiffiny**, Tiffney, Tifnee,
- **Thompson**, Tom, Tomás,
- **Tymothy**, Origin: Greek, Meaning: Honor to God, Blessed of God
- **Theodore,** Ted, Teddie,
- **Traciya,** Tracy, Tracya,
- **Tasmine**, Tasmin, Origin: English, Meaning: Twin, Worthy
- **Tarah**, Taira, Tairra,
- **Tanna**, Tannia, Tannis,
- **Tino**, Tíno, Origin: Hispanic, Meaning: Venerable, Promised Hope

- **Tina**, Teena, Téna, Tyna, Origin: English, Meaning: Anointed, Protected
- **Terry**, Therese, Thérese,
- **Trilby**, Trilbee, Trilbey,
- **Tobias**, Tobee, Tobey,
- **Toby,** Origin: Hebrew, Meaning: The Lord Is Good, God's Workmanship
- **Tiltan**, Tilton, Origin: Hebrew, Meaning: Clover, Blossom
- **Trixie**, Trix, Trixi, Origin: American, Meaning: Bringer of Joy, Peaceful

U

- **Ulric,** Ulrik, Origin: Old German, Meaning: Ruler of All, Regenerated
- **Ulrica**, Ulrika, Origin: Old German, Meaning: Ruler, Strong in Virtue
- **Ulani**, Ulana, Ulanna,
- **Uriah,** Urias, Uriyah, Origin: Hebrew, Meaning: God Is Light, Excellent Virtue
- **Uriel,** Uriela, Urieli,
- **Ulysses**, Ulisses, Origin: Latin, Meaning: One Who Detests, Seeker of Truth
- **Urbana,** Urbanna, Origin: Latin, Meaning: From the City, Majestic
- **Urban**, Urbain, Origin: Latin, Meaning: From the City, Peaceful
- **Uri**, Uree, Urii

V

- **Valerie**, Val, Valarae,
- **Virginia**, Virg, Origin: Virgenia, Latin, Meaning: Pure, Unblemished
- **Viktory**, Viktorya, Origin: Latin, Meaning: Conqueror, Triumphant Spirit
- **Valery,** Vallerie, Valllery,
- **Vallie**, Vally, Origin: Latin, Meaning: Strong, God's Leader
- **Viktoria**, Viktoriana,
- **Van**, Vann, Origin: Dutch, Meaning: Water Dam, Forgiving
- **Varina**, Vareena,
- **Valin**, Vaylin
- **Violet,** Vi, Viola, Violette,
- **Vicki,** Vickie, Vicky,
- **Vanissa,** Venessa, Origin: Greek, Meaning: Butterfly, Free Spirit
- **Vance**, Vanse, Origin: English, Meaning: Thresher, Hard Worker

- **Vallory**, Origin: Latin, Meaning: Strength, Spiritual Purpose
- **Verina**, Verity
- **Vivian**, Viv, Vivia,
- **Vlade**, Vladé, Origin: Russian, Meaning: Famous Prince, Upright
- **Veronica**, Varonica,
- **Veronika**, Véronique,
- **Vandie**, Vandda
- **Victor**, Vic, Victer, Vik,
- **Viktor**, Origin: Latin, Meaning: Conqueror, Triumphant Spirit
- **Venus,** Veenus, Origin: Latin, Meaning: Love, Greatest Power
- **Valerie**, Valeree, Valeri,
- **Vera**, Vara, Vira, Origin: Latin, Meaning: Truth, Strong in Virtue
- **Vianna**, Viana
- **Vivien**, Vivienne, Origin: Latin, Meaning: Lively Joyous Spirit
- **Vivana**, Vivianne,
- **Vanda**, Vandelia, Vandi,
- **Vanessa**, Vanesa,
- **Victoria**, Vicci, Vickee,

➤ **Vincent**, Vincente,

W

- **Welby**, Wellby, Origin: Old English, Meaning: From the Near Well, Trusting Spirit
- **Warner**,
- **William,** Bill, Billy, Wil,
- **Wynn,** Wyn, Wynette,
- **Whittney,** Witney,
- **Walter**, Walt, Origin: Old, German, Meaning: Powerful Ruler, Strong Protector
- **Willis,** Willus, Origin: English, Meaning: Son of the Guardian, Cautious
- **Walton**, Walt, Origin: English, Meaning: From the Fortified Town, Freedom of Spirit
- **Wynston**, Origin: Old English, Meaning: From the Friendly Town, Trusting
- **Wynnona**, Wynona, Origin: Sioux, Meaning: First-Born Daughter, Peaceful
- **Willow**, Wilow, Origin: English, Meaning: Willow Tree, Great Hope
- **Wynne**, Origin: Welsh, Meaning: Fair, Righteous
- **Wiley,** Will, Wiley, Willie,

- **Wyman,** Wymon, Origin: Old English, Meaning: Warrior, Determined
- **Wilhelm,** Willhelm, Origin: Old German, Meaning: Determined Guardian, Wise
- **Wendell,** Wendal,
- **Wendy**, Wenda,
- **Wagner,** Waggner, Origin: Old German, Meaning: Wagon Maker, Trusting Spirit
- **Wesley,** Wes, Weslee,
- **Walker**, Wallker, Origin: English, Meaning: Cloth Cleaner, Diligent
- **Wendi**, Wendie
- **Whitley**, Whitlee,
- **Wendee**, Wendey,
- **Weldon**, Welden, Origin: Old English, Meaning: From Hill Near the Well Preserved
- **Wyatt**, Wyat, Wyatte, Origin: Old French, Meaning: Little Warrior, Immoveable
- **Wallace**, Wallach,
- **Whitney**, Whitnee,
- **Whitnie**, Whittany,
- **Wallis**, Wally, Walsh,
- **Westlee**, Westley, Origin: English, Meaning: From the Western, Meadow Steadfast

- **Whitnée**, Whitneigh,
- **Willy,** Wilson, Origin: Old German, Meaning: Resolute Protector, Noble Spirit
- **Wade**, Wayde, Origin: Old English, Meaning: One Who Advances, Generous Spirit

X

- > **Xylina**, Origin: Greek, Meaning: Wood, One of Integrity
- > **Xandriana**, Xandria
- > **Xuan**, Xuann, Origin: Vietnamese, Meaning: Spring, Refreshed
- > **Xaven**, Xavon, Zavier,
- > **Xavier**, Xavian, Xavion,
- > **Xandra**, Xandraea,
- > **Xenia**, Xena
- > **Xylia**, Xyleah, Xyliana,
- > **Xuxa**, Xùxa, Origin: Brazilian, Meaning: Lily, Beautiful

Y

- **Yelina**, Yelana, Yelanna
- **Yago**, see Iago
- **Yasmine**, Yasmen,
- **Yannam**, Yannah,
- **Yves**, Ives, Origin: French, Meaning: Little Archer, Trusting Spirit
- **Yvonne**, Ivette, Ivonne,
- **Yadin**, Yadeen, Yadín, Origin: Hebrew, Meaning: God Will Judge, Righteous
- **Yarianna**, Yaryna, Origin: Russian, Meaning: Peace, Secure
- **Yul**, Yule, Yuul, Origin: Mongolian, Meaning: Beyond the Horizon, Worshiper
- **Yannika**, (see also Jana), Origin: Polish, Meaning: Gift of God, Purchased

Z

- **Zandra**, Zahndra,
- **Zena**, Zeena, Zeenia,
- **Zorina**, Zori, Zoriana,
- **Zachary**, Zachrey,
- **Zadok,** Zaydok, Origin: Hebrew, Meaning: Righteous, Rewarded
- **Zabrina**, Sabrina
- **Zephyr,** Zephria,
- **Zoee**, Zoey, Zoia, Zoie,
- **Zerlina**, Zerleyna, Origin: Spanish, Meaning: Dawn, Blessed
- **Zia**, Zea, Zeah, Zeya, Origin: Middle Eastern, Meaning: Light Fearless
- **Zacccary**, Zach,
- **Zephriana**, Origin: Greek, Meaning: West Wind, Reborn
- **Zeenya**, Zeina
- **Zacary**, Zacc, Zaccari,

- **Zuri**, Zuria, Zuriya, Origin: Swahili, Meaning: Beautiful, Messenger
- **Zephaniah**, Zephan,
- **Zaimir**, Zameer, Zameir, Origin: Hebrew, Meaning: Song, Joyful
- **Zacharee,** Zacharee,
- **Zackarie,** Zackary,
- **Zoe**, Zoa, Zöe, Zoé,
- **Zimra**, Zamora, Zemora, Origin: Hebrew, Meaning: Song of Praise, Thankful
- **Zoranna,** Zoriana,
- **Zackery**, Zackory,
- **Zaynah,** Zayna

Chapter 6 –Four Part Checklist for Testing the Name So You Can Know if It's the Right One

2. **Initials.** Think about the initial that will be created. Also, think about possible extended initials for email addresses. For example, the name Ajani Erkson can automatically become ajerk@stanford.com.

1. **Use your voice** Take the name through a verbal test. Names that can be subject to unwanted attention or mispronunciations can be wise to avoid.

3. **Think about your baby as an adult.** Bunny might be a cute name for a baby but what about an adult?

4. **Avoid overcomplicated names.** By choosing a simple name, you can avoid giving your child frustrating feelings. What can you do to minimize the chances of your child is going to have to say the phrase "Pardon me, my name is actually..."?

Conclusion

While being pregnant, some people love to ask questions about the name that you will give to your child. Some people might even offer you their own opinion regardless of whether or not it was asked for.

With the help of this book, you have hopefully discovered a few new names that you haven't thought about before. Perhaps you have already decided on the perfect name. Regardless of where you are at in your baby names journey, we want to thank you and offer you our best wishes for you and your family's future. Take care.

Write the names that you like here:

_____

_____

_____

_____

_____

_____

_____

_____

_____

_____

_____

_____

_____

_____

Made in the USA
San Bernardino, CA
29 January 2018